NSE, BUT DRAW THE LINE AT NUDE FOOTAGE • TODAY IS NOT A DRESS REHEARSAL

WS • SUIT YOURSELF • SOME STATEMENTS ARE MORE FASHION

SAY THEY'RE TIRED OF THE MEDIA'S OBSESSION WITH PO

AFERS • KEEP YOUR BEST FOOT FORWARD AND THE OTHER OU

E • THE AVERAGE WOMAN FALLS IN LOVE 7 TIMES A YEAR. ONLY 6 ARE WITH SHOES

% OF KIDS TODAY HAVE ACCESS TO THE HOTTEST NEW ACCESSORY. THE FAMILY GUN

N THEIR MATE • THESE ARE THE TIMES TO TRY MEN'S SOLES • GOD DRESS AMERICA!

BARE FEET • 39% OF WOMEN PREFER SHOE SHOPPING TO SEX • SOLE SEARCH

THEIR MARRIAGE • SUIT YOURSELF • TODAY IS NOT A DRESS REHEARSAL

NUDE FOOTAGE • IT'S OK TO BE CLOTHES MINDED • AVOID SPLINTERS WEAR SHOES

THAN OTHERS • SUIT YOURSELF • AVOID SPLINTERS WEAR SHOES • SOLE SEARCH

SAY THEY'RE TIRED OF THE MEDIA'S OBSESSION WITH POLITICAL SCANDAL

AFERS • KEEP YOUR BEST FOOT FORWARD AND THE OTHER OUT OF YOUR MOUTH

E • THE AVERAGE WOMAN FALLS IN LOVE 7 TIMES A YEAR. ONLY 6 ARE WITH SHOES

7% OF KIDS TODAY HAVE ACCESS TO THE HOTTEST NEW ACCESSORY. THE FAMILY GUN

N THEIR MATE • GOD DRESS AMERICA! • THESE ARE THE TIMES TO TRY MEN'S SOLES

FEET • STAND FOR SOMETHING OR STEP ASIDE • TODAY IS NOT A DRESS REHEARSAL

SUCCESS MAKING THEIR OUTFIT WORK THAN THEIR MARRIAGE • SUIT YOURSELF

E FOOTAGE • 55% OF SOCIETY BELIEVES THE MEDIA SHOULD FOCUS ON REAL NEWS

WEAR SHOES • TO BE AWARE IS MORE IMPORTANT THAN WHAT YOU WEAR

SHIRT • KEEP YOUR BEST FOOT FORWARD AND THE OTHER OUT OF YOUR MOUTH

AFERS • 1 IN 27 PEOPLE EXECUTED IN THE U.S. IS PROVEN INNOCENT OVER TIME

ST AS MANY SUITS ARE TRIED IN THE COURTROOM TODAY AS THE DRESSING ROOM

HESE ARE THE TIMES TO TRY MEN'S SOLES • STAND FOR SOMETHING OR STEP ASIDE

N THEIR MATE • SOLE SEARCH • AVOID SPLINTERS WEAR SHOES • SHIRT HAPPENS

CONDONE THE RIGHT TO BARE FEET • 39% OF WOMEN PREFER SHOE SHOPPING TO SEX

FOOTNOTES

Life has its bare essentials.
—Kenneth Cole

FOOTNOTES

WHAT YOU STAND FOR IS MORE IMPORTANT THAN WHAT YOU STAND IN

KENNETH COLE

WITH MIRA JACOB

Simon & Schuster
New York London Toronto Sydney Singapore

FOOTNOTES
—KENNETH COLE

OPEN AND CLOTHES

Kenneth Cole, the company, turned twenty years old in 2003.[1] In that time I've watched as it transformed itself from a good idea to a big, publicly traded organization with a life of its own. It's a business that I've run for many years, and now I wonder if it's somehow running me. Together, the company and I have lived through one unconventional debut, two trials of the century, four headquarters relocations, four United States Presidents (two Bushes), one Subway Series, fifteen full solar eclipses, thirty ad campaigns, eighty-plus nationwide store locations, and more than 7,300 days in the fashion industry. (Not to mention the sixth coming of platform shoes.)

People tell me that reflecting is what one does on such occasions: the older you get, apparently the more you are supposed to do it. I figure this is a good opportunity to address questions that, if they are not being asked of me, they are being asked *by* me. Why did I do this? Why am I still doing this? What is *this*? And how much caffeine must it all entail?

In the following pages I recount my entrepreneurial beginnings and some of our company's many adventures. It includes the story of an unlikely marriage between social responsibility and the business

LEFT: Fall 2001 runway show disclaimer.

of fashion; and how I discovered that the two are not mutually exclusive; in fact, they are interdependent. Even today, I know that much of what sustains this company is our belief that we're doing a lot more than just selling shoes, footwear, clothing, and accessories.

This is a story that is still in progress. I always thought that if I were ever going to tell it, it would be at a time when I was older and wiser. I guess I was assuming a lot. First, that age would confer wisdom, and second, that the story had to be finished in order to be his story.[2]

When people realize how long I've been doing this they sometimes ask if I've grown up in the business. To which I will often reply, "No, but I intend to." Throughout my career I have refused to look back, believing that exercise to be distracting and indulgent. I have always known that I can't allow myself to revel in the past, and yet, both its successes and its defeats have taught me valuable lessons. The ability to go forward depends upon my capacity to remember these lessons and at the same time to stay focused on what lies ahead. That is why I have included some of them here, in the form of footnotes to the Footnotes.

I've made my living in the fashion world where what is relevant is constantly open to interpretation. Yet the very nature of fashion is change, and if there is one thing I've learned in this business, it's that anything can change, and everything eventually will. Tomorrow can change everything, never mind the next twenty years. So with the power vested in some chosen words and selected images, here it is from beginning to middle . . .

FOOTNOTE #1
IT'S OUR AGE, NOT OUR SHOE SIZE

One could say that we were twenty *last* year (old enough to drive, but not to drink), because we incorporated in 1982. But since we didn't actually ship any shoes until the following spring, we decided to bend the truth and celebrate this milestone in 2003. Why not? Women have gotten away with lying about their age for years. Besides, in this business it's cooler to be younger anyway.

FOOTNOTE #2
PUN-TIFICATION

You will bear witness to many puns along the way, which I believe is the result of a preexisting condition. Although I have learned to temper it somewhat, I have come to accept it as an attempt by my brain to do with words what it also does with shapes and silhouettes.

LESSON: *When in doubt, pun-t.*

ALTHOUGH ALONE WE MAY NOT HEEL THE WORLD, WE HOPE TO BE AN ACCESSORY.

—KENNETH COLE

one

WHY FASHION IS ~~NOT~~ IMPORTANT

Even after twenty years in fashion, I do not consider myself an expert on the subject, and the views I express don't necessarily apply to other designers. My understanding of trends has evolved as much from the world at large as it has from the fashion world. And to those experts on fashion and culture who hold different views, well, I fully defend their right to disagree.

That said, of course fashion is important! Though often considered trivial, fashion in many ways defines the moment, and reflects the cultural tone of the times. At the same time, fashion is utterly subjective, and deeply personal, affecting and influencing everyone differently. It has even been said to provide some shoppers with a sense of euphoria usually experienced only by intravenous drug users.

I spend a major part of my waking (i.e., working) hours making things that no one needs, but fortunately for me, many think they do. I've come to realize that my job is to inspire the customer to proceed from desire to purchase—to make a customer want to buy his twenty-fifth tie, because this new one is a little wider; or her *eighth* white shirt, because of its fit; or, I hope, a *thirty-sixth* pair of shoes, because the heel is the right height, and because there is nothing like a new pair of shoes. Nonetheless, I know perfectly well that if every shoe store in America closed its doors tomorrow, hardly an American would go barefoot for at least eleven years.

I live the business of fashion and, as businesses go, it's a tough one. It's difficult because it's about form as well as function, and because it's not just about what is there, but also what is not, and *that* is forever changing. Even if you're on the right track in this business, if you aren't moving fast enough, you still risk getting hit by the next train.

Although fashion may not seem profound in and of itself, it's certainly an important and alluring medium: a social and political mirror, a reflection of how we feel about our community and our life in general. Fashion tells us who we are, individually and collectively, at any given point in time. Take women's clothing. The cut of

RIGHT: Fall 1998 national ad campaign.

12

YOU ARE ON A VIDEO CAMERA
AN AVERAGE OF 10 TIMES A DAY.
ARE YOU DRESSED FOR IT?
—KENNETH COLE

FOOTNOTE #3
WHAT'S IN A NAME

My situation is unusual in that, even though most people know my name, few people recognize me.

One night over dinner, my daughter Amanda asked me if I was famous. I am not famous, I told her. But my name is. Why? She said that when people met her they often asked if she was Kenneth Cole's daughter, and it made her feel strange. Hey, I thought to myself, it's better than being Hannibal Lecter's daughter! But her sisters had nodded when she brought it up, as though this was a shared problem, one we needed to address.

Until someone knows you, I told them, they are going to define you by what they know about you. But the more they get to know you, the more they don't care about that stuff. Although that day you were Amanda, Kenneth Cole's daughter, tomorrow you could be Amanda, Emily's younger sister, and the next you could be Amanda, the smart kid with the blue knapsack.

In my case, although my name appears on lots of products in lots of places, I still have my privacy most of the time, and can also get a reservation in most restaurants. So I guess we just take the good with the bad.

LESSON: First *impressions needn't* last.

women's garments says a lot about how women in society feel and how they are perceived. From the flowing bell-bottoms of the 1960s, to the ultra-feminine dresses of the 1970s, to the androgynous power suits of the 1980s, women's clothing tells a story. What does it mean that in the late 1990s, successful women no longer had to dress like men to prove their competence? Nothing, on one level, but a whole lot on another.

As individuals we use fashion to define ourselves and tell the world who we are. When we get up in the morning, what we put on is very much a reflection of how we see the world and how we want it to see us. Our bodies become our own medium for communication, and every day becomes a chance to reintroduce ourselves to the universe. No one can deny that people's perceptions of us are influenced by what they know about us.[3] Often all that we know about someone is how they have chosen to present themselves; how they dye their hair, where they apply their tattoos, or what they have decided to wear is often all that we have to work with. We can't always control the reality of our life the way we can control the perception of it. We are given an uncensored opportunity, every day, to be who we want to be.

Since fashion is an extraordinary force that means different things to different people, it not only plays a role in our aesthetic existence but in our emotional well-being. It can truly affect how we feel throughout our day. How many times have you heard someone say, I was down in the dumps, so I bought these shoes? (How many times have you felt like answering: I always wondered where and why you bought them.)

I've always believed that how you look is a self-fulfilling prophecy: when you wake up, get dressed, and look in the mirror, if you think you look good, most likely you will. You'll probably smile more and be more at ease. On the other hand, thinking you look bad, or are dressed inappropriately for what the day has in store, can have the opposite effect.

I find creative energy at every level of the fashion business, from the designing to the marketing. Like an artist I have a canvas; mine just happens to come in pairs, and lengths, and different fabrics. And when

West Germany, 1968

"No, we said accessorize."
-Kenneth Cole

NEW YORK TIMES

ALL THE NEWS THAT'S FIT TO PRINT, AND THEN SOME. FROM 1997 TO 1999 WE RAN A BI-WEEKLY AD
THE NEWS . . . JUST IN CASE ANYONE ACTUALLY WANTED OUR OPINION.

1/14/97
Mike Tyson was clearly
hungry for the
heavyweight title.

4/27/97
The economy is falling,
Iraq is a threat
and Ellen is gay.
Is there a problem here?

8/17/97
UPS went on strike
and the nation
was at a stand-still.

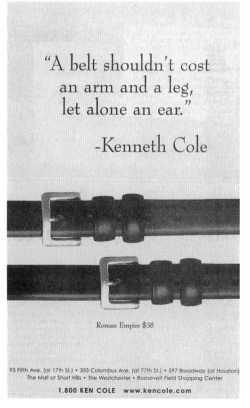

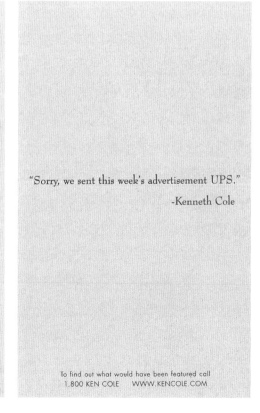

11/09/97
Not only does
fashion repeat itself,
unfortunately history
does too.

5/17/98
It was the moment men
had been waiting for;
clothing arrived at our
5th Avenue store.
Oh, and Viagra arrived
on the market.

8/27/98
Russia is in turmoil,
the people take
to the streets and
their leader
takes to the bottle.

"If only Mr.
Hussein had been
given a bigger boot
the last time."

-Kenneth Cole

Flat Tax
$148

95 Fifth Ave. (at 17th St.) • 353 Columbus Ave. (at 77th St.) • 597 Broadway (at Houston)
The Mall at Short Hills • The Westchester • Roosevelt Field Shopping Center

1.800 KEN COLE   www.kencole.com

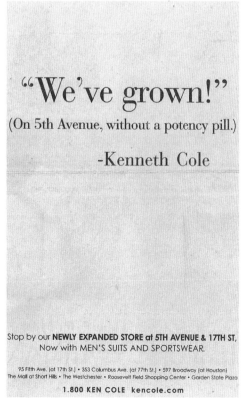

"We've grown!"
(On 5th Avenue, without a potency pill.)

-Kenneth Cole

Stop by our **NEWLY EXPANDED STORE** at **5TH AVENUE & 17TH ST,**
Now with MEN'S SUITS AND SPORTSWEAR.

95 Fifth Ave. (at 17th St.) • 353 Columbus Ave. (at 77th St.) • 597 Broadway (at Houston)
The Mall at Short Hills • The Westchester • Roosevelt Field Shopping Center • Garden State Plaza

1.800 KEN COLE   kencole.com

"Dear Mr. Yeltsin:
Firing your entire cabinet
is one way to get change.
Here's another."

-Kenneth Cole

Women's wallet $42.

KENCOLE.COM   1.800 KEN COLE

95 Fifth Ave. (at 17th St.) • 353 Columbus Ave. (at 77th St.)
597 Broadway (at Houston) • Roosevelt Field Shopping Center
The Westchester • The Mall at Short Hills • Garden State Plaza

AS WE ENTERED NEW MARKETS AND EXPANDED OUR RETAIL PRESENCE
IT SEEMED ONLY APPROPRIATE TO INTRODUCE OURSELVES.

OPENING IN NEW YORK CITY 1994

Who is Kenneth Cole, anyway?

Jay - Bellhop/Model, Manhattan

"If he's who I think he is,
he owes me five bucks."

Grace - Homemaker, Queens

"I think I roomed with him back
in college."

Mario - Governor, Albany

"Why, is he in the race now too?"

OPENING IN WASHINGTON DC 1995

What's Kenneth Cole doing in Pentagon City?

Dan - FBI

"If I told you I'd have to kill you."

Milton - CIA

"Why do you want to know? Who
sent you? Who are you working for?"

Boris - KGB

"The rooster's left shoe is facing west."

18

I've done my job well, when I've designed something like no other something, it's personally rewarding. In fact, when I see someone on the street wearing something I've made, there's this inner thrill, a sense of connection, a feeling that I know them, and can imagine how they feel about themselves. The customer and I have something in common. They usually don't recognize me, and yet I feel I know them. I look at them a second time, to understand better who my customer is. I'm curious; and, if they're not wearing my stuff, well, I'm curious about that, too. So if you see a dark-haired man dressed just like you on New York City's streets staring intently at your shoes, your belt buckle, or your raincoat, don't panic—he's probably either on his way to therapy, out on parole, or . . . it's just me.

So what could be more important than fashion?

Depending upon your circumstances, just about everything. Try shelter. If you don't have a place to sleep for the night, are you really going to be worried about what you look like? After all, fashion is just clothes, just shoes—fashion doesn't really change the world.

From the time I started our company, I've looked for ways to make what we do about something more than what we wear. And like most people, I was also searching for something to make my life more meaningful. After all, fashion alone is not enough of a reason to get up in the morning. It's certainly not a reason to leave my wife and kids to go to work every day for long hours, and to ask my associates for the required spirit to do the same. If what we do is only about fashion, I don't believe that the collective energy necessary for our success can be sustained.

So I started doing something that I thought might help the company truly help others. I began an advertising campaign that had more to do with raising awareness about social issues than it did about raising awareness of personal style. In the beginning, what we did was very simple and it didn't have a name. Since that time, we've been credited as one of the first companies to implement "cause-related marketing."

Because I believe our business depends on our understanding the whole person, we started a dialogue with our customers. If we truly wish to add value to their lives, we need to know what they care about and think about, as well as what they say and why they say it, how they feel and when, what they wear and why. We need to know what shapes their lives before we can understand their decision-making process. For if we know how they feel at any given point in time, and what is driving their emotions, we are more likely to know how to satisfy them.

Now, is it wise for a fashion company to address what's going on inside the customer? Some critics say no. And the truth is, often it isn't prudent to involve oneself in the social fiber of a community, which is far more complex than any business. Those same critics will usually say that a private business could never do anything that isn't self-serving. My answer to that is simple: of course I have a responsibility to

1988
THE AIDS EPIDEMIC FURTHER INFILTRATED OUR LIVES, AND REDEFINED OUR FUTURE.

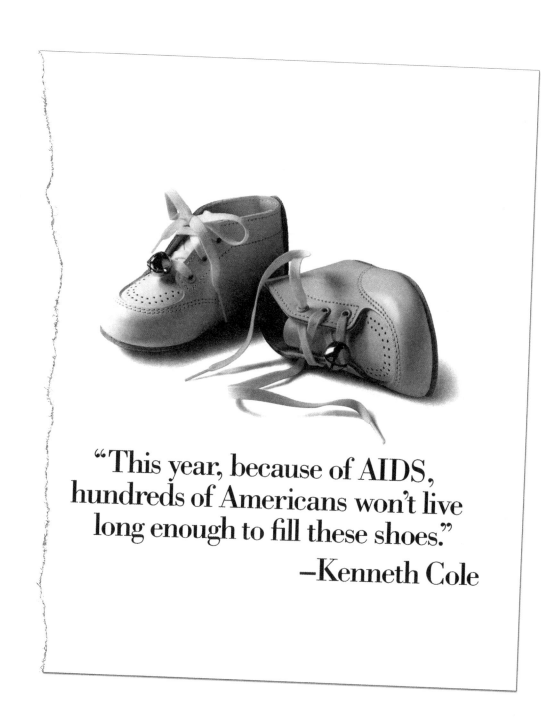

"This year, because of AIDS, hundreds of Americans won't live long enough to fill these shoes."

–Kenneth Cole

1993 FIVE YEARS LATER, CHANGE WAS SMALL IN SOME WAYS, BUT VERY BIG IN OTHERS.

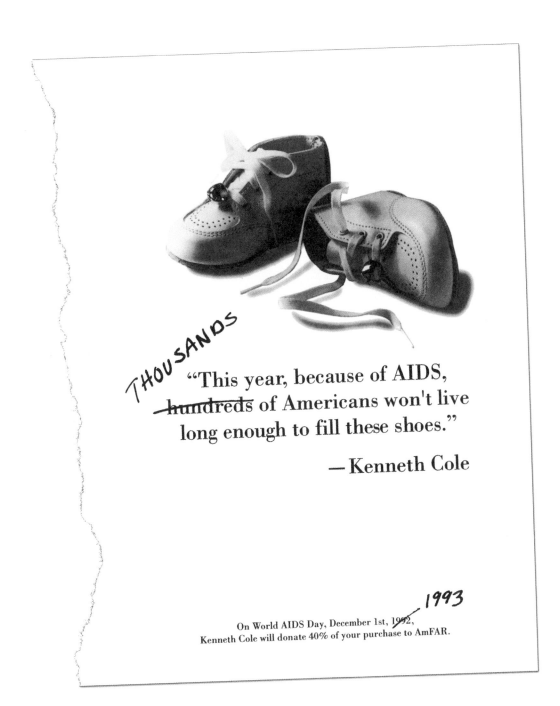

THOUSANDS

"This year, because of AIDS, ~~hundreds~~ of Americans won't live long enough to fill these shoes."

—Kenneth Cole

1993

On World AIDS Day, December 1st, 1992, Kenneth Cole will donate 40% of your purchase to AmFAR.

FOOTNOTE #4
A ROSE BY ANY OTHER NAME

By 1992, when Mario Cuomo, my father-in-law, had been governor of New York for twelve years, he decided to run for a fourth term. We had every reason to believe he would win; though the campaign had been difficult and dirty, he was still six points up in the polls as late as election morning. Maria and I decided to bring our daughters into the city to experience the excitement of election evening believing they would remember it for their lifetimes.

Around 7:00 P.M., watching the returns with the family and friends, we were shocked by the exit polls. We couldn't believe it, but by eight o'clock it was obvious that Mario had lost.

It was clear there was not going to be an acceptance speech, no big celebration welcoming another term. We were stunned. It was as if all of us, the family and the campaign staff workers and supporters, had run full force into a wall. To ensure that the night not become a traumatic memory for the girls, we helped them into their pajamas and put them to bed shortly after. At about ten, the governor—far more composed than anyone else—made an extraordinarily gracious and inspiring concession speech. Then we all returned to the suite.

At about six in the morning, I woke up to someone tapping me on the shoulder. Four-year-old Amanda was standing at the side of my bed.

She peered down at me and said, "Daddy, did Grandpa win?"

I said, "No."

She nodded. "Does that mean that he isn't going to be governor anymore?"

I nodded. "That's right. He's not going to be governor."

Then she asked, "Well, is he still going to be my grandpa?"

I looked at her for a minute, a little baffled. And responded, "Of course he is."

Her response was, "Well then, why is everybody so upset?"

Amanda's response, simple but poignant, snapped me back to reality. It was a conversation I reflect on often. As adults, we have such a marvelous ability to lose perspective on what's important. **LESSON:** *We tend to get so wrapped up in our myopic universe that we lose sight of who we are and what really matters.*

the company and its shareholders. And it's true that Kenneth Cole, the man, has benefited from our advertising as much as Kenneth Cole, the company. But more importantly, American Foundation for AIDS Research (amfAR), HELP USA, the Brady campaign for handgun control, and the people these organizations serve have benefited as well, and maybe more.

This is a very real conflict for me. I am sometimes reluctant to admit that involving ourselves in social causes is actually good for business. Profit, should it come, happens to be a fringe benefit, and while it's not why we do it, it *is* the reason we can keep on doing it. But in saying that, we are in danger of appearing insincere, or worse, of trivializing the issues.

But on this point I am reassured by all the encouragement we receive, both from the public and the fashion industry. a recent cover story in *Women's Wear Daily* (March 5, 2003) cited the top industry market researcher, NPDFashionworld: "Kenneth Cole leads a list of brands perceived by teens as 'prestigious,' followed by Donna Karan, Victoria's Secret, Ann Taylor, Liz Claiborne, Banana Republic, and Ralph Lauren," as well as Calvin Klein, Prada, and Gucci. The article observed that "Today, it's more about *being associated with a larger cause.* Kenneth Cole has done this better than anyone else in the past 20 years."

I believe that, if channeled correctly, a seemingly frivolous medium like fashion can become an important conduit for change. And if all we have done is to remind ourselves to keep it all in perspective, well, even that will have been more than we ever hoped for.

ENGLAND, 1984

"It's a rare occasion when we don't
have shoes to match your gown."

—Kenneth Cole

"Lights, camera, shoe-t!"

two

GROWING UP IN A TRAILER

I knew when I started Kenneth Cole Productions that, if I didn't do it then, I probably never would. Life would only get more complicated. From the beginning all of my resources, both financial and emotional, were brought to bear on the company. So when I am asked the question, "What would you have done if it *hadn't* worked?" I usually respond, at the risk of sounding flippant, "I *always* knew it would work. I just wasn't sure what 'it' was."

From my first youthful entrepreneurial enterprise at Shea Stadium, to working with my father at his shoe factory, to then launching my own company, "it" has changed in more ways than I thought possible.

There were other things I wanted to do when I grew up. I considered being President: I thought about the perks, like flying in Air Force One and never having to say I'm sorry, but then I mulled over the degree of responsibility, such as having to decide which country to bomb and who should sleep in Lincoln's bed. So I decided playing shortstop for the Mets would be far more enjoyable. My first job, selling peanuts in Shea Stadium, put me close enough to the playing field to envision myself on it.[5] I knew the game, I knew the crowd, and I knew the uniform would fit. There were two problems: I could neither hit far enough nor run fast enough. After high school, and four years of college, and a reality check, I figured that a legal education would give me a better foundation for whatever opportunities life would offer. I decided I wanted to be a lawyer, and prepared to head in that direction.

LEFT: Catalog cover, Fall, 1995.

FOOTNOTE #5
TO BE SUCCESSFUL *SOMETIMES* ∧ YOU HAVE TO BE NUTS

Someone once said, "If you do what you love and you love what you do, you'll never have to work a day in your life."

So what was the *ideal* reality for a boy from Long Island who spent his days living and breathing sports? What else but working at Shea Stadium, being able to see any game and maybe get paid at the same time. But this job wasn't just peanuts. After all, this wasn't just any game; it was the 1969 World Series. And it wasn't just any team; it was the Mets. They were up against the heavily favored Orioles, who had Frank Robinson and Boog Powell. At the time, the Mets had Tom Seaver, Cleon Jones, and Ron Swoboda. And the Mets also had a problem.

I heard about their problem at school one day that fall from a friend named Kip. Apparently, all the games in the World Series were going to be day games, and because of new truancy laws in the New York City schools, the Mets might not have enough vendors at the games. I had a great idea: they were short on vendors and I was long on reasons to see the World Series.

The concessions were run by a company called Harry M. Stevens, so we called and inquired about how to get a job. Apparently the Department of Education had a minor rule that stated any kid who wanted to cut school to work needed a note from their principal. The next stop, then, was the principal's office. We went in and talked to Mr. Elliot Noys about the cultural value experiencing the World Series would have for young men like ourselves. The principal was a sympathetic Mets fan, so he signed on. The rest happened quickly: we went down, applied for the job, and got it.

Short of a date with Raquel Welch, this was the best possible thing I could have ever imagined happening in my fifteen-year-old universe. I had a rotating seat at the World Series, and was the envy of every kid in my town. It was heaven.

There was just one little hitch that I hadn't seen coming. Until that point I hadn't really given much thought to the money I would make selling peanuts. Most of the other kids vending, on the other hand, had. They were off in the corner pitching quarters much of the time, trying to make even more. But once I got out there and realized that, with a little speed and agility, I could do pretty well, everything changed. I still love baseball, and I still love the Mets. But this job defined competition for me in a new way: I loved the business side, too.

I couldn't have guessed what happened next. The more I hustled, the more I liked selling peanuts; and the better I got, the better the seating sections allocated to me. My sections got closer to the field every day. As the Mets became the Miracle Mets, I became the Peanut Specialist. I was fast, I was smooth, slicker with every game. Tommie Agee caught a line drive by Elrod Hendricks while I gave out change with one hand and tossed bags with the other. Swoboda was saving Game 4 with a ninth-inning catch and I was throwing peanuts ten rows down and fifteen over—left, right, left. I was selling as many nuts as anyone, at which point it dawned on me that something about me had suddenly changed, maybe forever.

The Series was soon over, but the experience was not. The next season I worked the Jets games, before reaching the zenith of peanut salesmanship, the prize gig, the brass ring: Madison Square Garden for the Rangers and Knicks games. Now I was perplexed. Was I so intent on doing this well because it was challenging? Because, without anyone's help, I was now able to see every local sports team whenever I wanted? Or because of the opportunity to earn money and independence? Or all of the above?

I could have everything, I realized there and then: I could see the games, and make money, and have fun in an unexpected way. And therein was born an entrepreneur. From this I drew a **LESSON:** *that my passions could serve all kinds of needs and create new ones I didn't know I had.*

Home from Emory University with a B.A. and ready for law school in the fall, everything changed. For years, my father had owned and operated a woman's shoe factory, called El Greco, in Williamsburg, Brooklyn. That spring, my father's business manager, Bernie Mev, quit to start his own business. Suddenly my family's only source of income—literally the hand that fed us—appeared to be in jeopardy. Someone was needed to fill those shoes or at least knew how they felt.

I had already spent a few summers in Brooklyn working with my father, Charlie, a strong-willed ex-marine whose spirit and enthusiasm was infectious. I was intrigued by the passion he showed for his job: every working day the man was *thrilled* to be in a women's shoe factory. I couldn't imagine where this eccentric drive of his came from, but that summer I was determined to learn—along with everything else I would need to know about the shoe business. Wheeling a second desk into his own office, my father said: "Kenny, I want you to sit in on meetings, listen to conversations, hear how I talk to people, learn what I do. Just be there."

I knew I couldn't just be the boss's son: I needed to create my own place quickly. The only way to do that was to work harder than anyone else or, at the very least, to seem to. I knew that, at the start, the quantity of my work would count more than its quality, so I put in the hours.

In general, a shoe factory isn't a great environment to nourish an entrepreneur's drive. A factory is a place where restrictions prevail. From the four walls that enclose it and the ceiling that looms overhead, it's rarely the most conducive creative atmosphere (even in Williamsburg, Brooklyn, twenty years later the Rive Gauche of the art scene in New York). There are so many things that can go wrong—floods, fires, electrical shortages. Even on its very best day, the factory will only produce a finite number of items. An unlimited downside with a limited upside just didn't make good business sense, and I knew instinctively that the formula needed revision.

In the course of those long days and nights, I found myself gravitating to the very heart of the factory—the sample room. A sample room is to the shoe business what a kitchen is to a restaurant: it's the place where the product is conceived and where the recipe for the company's future success is created and ultimately executed. The possibilities for success, emanating from what began in the sample room, are then limited only by consumer demand, technical boundaries, and one's own imagination.

If I were going to play a role in that part of the process, I needed to be able to make the shoe myself, or sketch it for whoever would. So I taught myself to do both. Soon I could draw shoes from every angle, cut the pattern, and create the initial prototype. As children we are taught to draw within the lines; later in life I learned that the more creative you can be outside the boundaries, the better the results. I marveled at how a piece of leather and a variety of other assorted items (heels, buckles, laces), when con-

FOOTNOTE #6
THE RULES RULE

Every Friday there was a visitor to the factory named David, a low-key, heavyset man who had a store in lower Manhattan, a pocket full of cash, and a gun—licensed, I suppose, because he carried all that cash. Charlie, my father, would sell shoes to David for cash on the spot. For us, it was a quick way to move any surplus inventory; for David, it was a way to get a product he may not have otherwise been able to get. Whether or not he recorded the transaction was his business (and maybe even an important part of it).

David would arrive for his meeting with my father, and I'd follow them to the warehouse out back. Every week, my father paused and, in a grave voice, he began something like this: "David, business is great. I have three-hundred-some-odd pairs of shoes, but I don't really have them because Bloomingdale's wants them tomorrow. Then there's an ad that's going to break, and Nordstrom wants some, too. Now, because it's you, I'll give you the shoes, but this week I can't give them to you for eight dollars. I have to sell them for ten."

Looking pained, David would adopt an equally serious demeanor and reply, "Charlie, you know what? I haven't even sold what I bought last week. So frankly, I can't pay you eight dollars like I did last week, I can only pay you six."

They would go on like this for a while, elaborating here and there. Half an hour later, David would buy all the shoes available for eight dollars. He would count out the cash and leave. It happened every week. The stories changed from time to time, but when they were finished, David bought every pair of shoes we had left for eight dollars. And week after week, I was the only witness to this ancient ritual.

At the end of my first summer there, when my father went on vacation, he asked me to deal with David. "You know how it works, and David trusts you." By that time, I was coordinating sample production and slipping in a few of my own designs. I had a lot to do, but I did know David, so I said, "Sure."

On Friday, when David appeared at the front desk, I greeted him, saying, "My father isn't here, but I can work with you."

"Okay," David answered, "but I don't have a lot of time."

When we got to the stockroom I said, "David, you know, I've watched this now for eight weeks in a row. I've seen how my father starts and I've seen how you start. He sits here and tells you that he didn't need to sell the shoes. He gives you the speech, and at the end he tells you we need to sell them to you for ten dollars. And then you say you need to buy them for six. And in half an hour you pay him eight dollars and leave. Now, the problem is I'm doing both his job and mine, and I don't *have* half an hour. So why don't we skip the back-and-forth part, and you just pay me the same eight dollars you paid for the same shoes for the last eight weeks? Look, I have the shoes all ready for you."

David listened to me in silence. "You know, Kenny," he said at last, "the thing is, I got more inventory than I've had in the past. I can only pay four dollars this week."

I stared in disbelief. "David, you can't be serious! Why are you doing this? I know how this works. I just don't have time to negotiate."

With that, David left. For the first time in the many years that he and my father had done business, he walked out without buying shoes.

I learned something from what didn't happen. I learned that if you're going to do business, you have to learn the rules. Before I went into the factory that day, I knew that David had only done business one way. What I didn't know was that there was only one way David *would* do business. After my attempt to change the rules, I had to ask myself if I really wanted to do business with David at all.

For my father, the answer to that question was emphatically yes. For me, the answer was emphatically maybe.

The **LESSON** was, *I need to know whom I'm dealing with, and what the rules are.*

Whether I chose to play by them, of course, is another matter entirely.

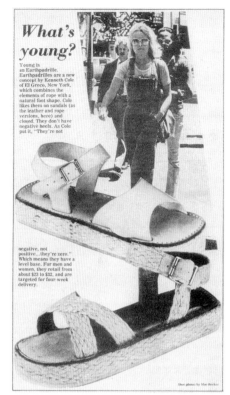

FOOTWEAR NEWS
1976 cover story of a new product by some unknown designer.

Below: Charles Cole and bearded apprentice in Milan, September 1980.

FOOTNOTE #7
IF YOU BUILD IT . . .

At one point, we were trying to get financing from our bank, Irving Trust, and our account manager came to the factory and sat down in our office. This is the kind of meeting for which most people in business would have prepared elaborate spreadsheets to clearly illustrate their need.

The manager asked about our open order position, or how much demand there was for our product. "About three inches," I replied.

"What?" he asked, baffled.

I pointed to the orders basket on my desk. "Three inches thick," I clarified. "We have orders for 200 percent more than we can fulfill, and we are selling them for three times the price that we are paying for them." To complicate matters, we were so disorganized that we were occasionally shipping people two to three times off the same order, whereas customers would usually return anything not ordered, now they were calling up to say, "Thank you."

In any case we got the financing we needed and the stores (our customers) eagerly accommodated our operational inefficiencies.

LESSON: *The bigger message here for me was that if you build the field, and it is the right field, they will come.*

structed the right way, materialized into a shoe. I was totally mesmerized by how, with the slightest variation, I had a different shoe entirely. And with that, my own creative journey began.

Creativity has always intrigued me. It is a lofty term, right up there with "artist" and "genius." Like a lot of people, I considered creativity a gift you either had or you didn't. It came from the heavens, arriving with a ray of light and a few singing cherubs. It seemed to visit SoHo more often than Brooklyn. What I was doing across the East River in Brooklyn seemed too, well, logical to be creative. I had specific variables I was working with. I had to figure out what shoes people wanted and what options already existed; then I could explore creative alternatives within defined technical boundaries.

My first work came out of this process. In 1976, espadrilles were one of the hottest trends; the other was a "negative-heel" shoe called an Earth Shoe. I took the negative-heel concept, mixed the sole with jute, and the result was a round-toed shoe and sandal with a rope base that I called Earthpadrilles. Within a week they were featured on the cover of the industry's leading trade publication, *Footwear News* magazine. (The article by Vivian Infantino even called me an up-and-coming "designer." See p. 29)

I had only been in the business for a month, but I was hooked: the entire process was gratifying beyond words. My ambitions as a lawyer were put on the same shelf as the dream of playing shortstop for the Mets. I suddenly found myself considering a very different journey—in women's footwear, no less.

Meanwhile, back in Williamsburg and the factory, I was exposed to more and more of the operation of the shoe business. Sitting at the desk in my father's office, I often learned what to do from him and, just as importantly, what *not* to do.[6] After two years of working together, we came out with an overseas import called Candie's. When launched, Candie's were unlike any other presumed-to-be-wooden-heeled shoes on the market. The synthetic substance used to make them was less expensive than traditional materials, so they could be made cheaply, sold for three times what it cost us to manufacture them, and still cost less than existing alternatives. Better yet, because we introduced them to the marketplace, we set the standard for this style of sandal. Because price and value are

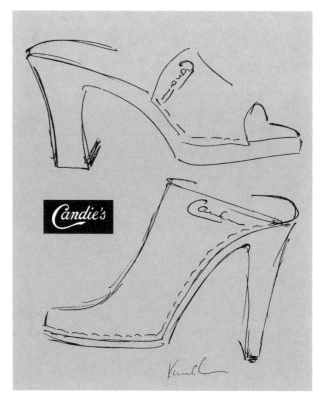

Circa 1978—Candie's

relative (something is expensive only if there is a similar product that costs less), the value of Candie's was ours to determine. Candie's high-heeled, backless shoes were enormously popular. Over time, I have come to accept that we may have crippled half a generation of female Americans. Eventually, the rapid expansion of the business caught up to us. As we sought to enlarge the points of distribution, we were forced to compromise the quality of our distribution. In just four years our business had gone from $5 million in sales to nearly $80 million. When the company expanded, we were joined by my brother Neil (who actually did go to law school, and later became an important part of all that followed), and then by my youngest brother, Evan, a great salesman, and my sister, Abbie, with her wonderful sense of style. We clearly had the right product, but we also had a minimal infrastructure, and never enough financing.[7]

Around this time, it was becoming obvious to me that my father's business sense was in many ways different from mine. After a few years, our business philosophies had diverged, and I realized that we were too different to manage the same company. He had a more traditional outlook on business, believing, for example, that advertising was a sign of weakness, and that placing an ad was as good as saying we didn't have confidence in our product's ability to sell itself. He also believed a bigger company was automatically a better company, and any press was good press.

I had other ideas. After months of thinking things through, I made the difficult decision to leave. I discussed the matter with my father, who listened carefully. "I hope you have enough money," he said. "It's not that easy out there." He paused. Then he added, "You'll be back."

With those words, I heard the door shut firmly behind me. He went on to say that he would keep my office empty so that it would be easy for me to return, and I know that he meant it in a loving way. Still, it was in that instant I knew I would never go back.

Leaving the family business put me in a catch-22. I needed to succeed immediately at whatever business I started, since I didn't have the resources to finance a second try; in fact, I barely had enough for a first. But success in the only business I was really experienced in would put me in direct competition with my family. Therefore, to do well *and* feel good about it, I needed to make different kinds of shoes without taking any employees away from the family business, and I stood by that. But I did bring along my good friend, Sam Edelman, who wouldn't have it any other way, and who was an important part of my start-up.

I knew I had to distinguish myself and step out in a direction I had never taken before. I needed to be a different kind of a shoe person with a different kind of company. And while that was a little unnerving, I felt in my bones that "it"—whatever "it" was—had to change, and that I would have to change, too.

I decided to aim high—for the fashion elite, the trendsetters, the club crowd, confident that selling to them would not affect Candie's, and knowing that, once I sold to them, I could sell to anyone. These were women who would buy a pair of shoes before they'd paid their rent, who spent their days at work and their nights at Studio 54. Most people I knew either wanted to date them or be them. I just wanted to sell them shoes.

But how? I had limited money and very little time. I knew the basic danger, that most businesses run out of capital before they can generate cash flow. I needed to get started, but first I had to decide on a name; I needed to create business cards, signage, boxes, and stationery right away. I couldn't, however, take the chance of registering a company name and finding out months later it wasn't valid—but I knew I could get an individual's name registered. So I used the one my parents had come up with twenty-some years prior, and the certificate of incorporation for Kenneth Cole Incorporated was filed in September of 1982, printed across business cards and packaging, and registered in the upcoming trade show.

Next, I was going to need financing. I knew it was going to be easier to get credit from shoe factories in Italy that needed business than from American banks that didn't. I found an agent, lined up the factories, and headed to Florence, Italy. I then designed a collection of shoes in the factories, and returned to the States, ready to sell them.

The footwear industry, like most, has "market weeks"—days when the industry comes together to view its options. Buyers from the nation's various stores would arrive in New York and converge at the Hilton Hotel to see what more than 1,100 small- to medium-sized footwear companies have to offer (invariably one-thousand-plus varieties of the same things). The larger and more established companies, however, exhibit in permanent showrooms within a four-block radius of the Hilton.

I had reservations about both of these options. A hotel room didn't offer a lot of personality, or individuality, and worse, I couldn't afford it. The larger showrooms promised more identity, but also far more expense, and I *really* couldn't afford them and even if I could, I didn't have the time.

I was out of options, but not ideas. Where else could I gain access to the buyers and not be beholden to either of the current alternatives? I quickly realized I had to do something between the hotel and the showrooms. Somewhere on the street.

On a whim, I called a friend in the trucking business and asked if I could borrow one of his trailers to park it on 56th Street and Sixth Avenue, two blocks from the Hilton and in front of a fancy shoe building. "Sure, but good luck getting permission," he said. "This is New York. You can't park a bicycle there for four minutes, let alone a truck for four days."

So I called the mayor's office, Mayor Koch at the time, and asked how one gets permission to park a forty-foot trailer truck in midtown Manhattan. They said, emphatically, one doesn't. They explained that the city only gave parking permits to utility companies servicing the streets, like Con Ed or AT&T, or to production companies shooting full-length motion pictures. (The "I love New York" campaign was in full force in the early 1980s and the city was anxious to attract movie business.) So that day I ran to the stationery store and changed our company letterhead from Kenneth Cole, Inc. to Kenneth

"Ah...Ah...Ahh...Shoe!"
—Kenneth Cole

"A Free What?"
—Kenneth Cole

Cole Productions, Inc. The next day I applied for a permit to shoot a full-length motion picture entitled *The Birth of a Shoe Company*.

With Kenneth Cole Productions painted on the side of the truck, we opened for business on December 2, 1982, in front of 1370 Avenue of the Americas. Surrounded by the big company showrooms, two blocks north of the Hilton, we had a fully furnished forty-foot trailer, klieg lights, a director, a rolling camera (sometimes there was even film in it), models as actresses, and two of New York's Finest (policemen) as doormen—compliments of Mayor Ed Koch. Soon, we even had crowds. A velvet rope allowed a limited number of people in the trailer. There wasn't an important buyer in our industry that didn't come to see us in those few days. Most of them were forced to wait. The longer they waited, the more anxious they were to get in, and invariably the bigger their eventual order. We sold forty thousand pairs of shoes in three and a half days and were off and running.

To this day the company is still named Kenneth Cole Productions, Inc., and is traded on the New York Stock Exchange as KCP. It reminds us of how we came to be and serves as a reminder of the importance of resourcefulness and innovative problem solving, proof that the best solution is not always the most expensive, but usually the most creative.

SCENES FROM
"BIRTH OF A
SHOE COMPANY"
A Kenneth Cole Production
**The trailer contained shoes
and the camera contained
film...sometimes.**

three

ACT I, SCENE II:
THE SHOE MUST GO ON

They say that a trip of a thousand miles begins with the first step. After our debut at the semiannual Shoe Show, our company began its thousand-mile journey. Since the beginning it was clear that nothing would meet customers' expectations better than the unexpected, so we set out to bring it to them. Our product needed to be different from the existing alternatives, and so did we.

First, there were some basic logistics to deal with. For a few months after our debut, the business operated entirely out of my apartment on the East Side of Manhattan. The living room became the showroom, the paperwork was spread out on the dinner table, and the bedroom served as my executive enclave. Sam came every morning, and my second employee, Vincent Cavallero[8], did the same. Obviously we needed a larger space—preferably one I wasn't living in. Between working and sleeping and ordering in Chinese food, I often remained in the building for days on end. It scared everyone a little. I was turning into an entrepreneurial recluse—a younger, less wealthy, but better-dressed Howard Hughes. I left the office/apartment only for trips abroad, to design the collections and check production in small, provincial factories outside Tuscany, and along the Adriatic coast. When asked what I did in my spare time, I'd often reply, "Fasten my seat belt and put my seat back and tray table in their original upright position."

Six months after our first Shoe Show, by unanimous consent KCP made the ultimate commitment: office space in New York City. The overhead was scary. I had always known that as long as I kept my expenses variable I couldn't lose. If we did a lot of business, we stood to make a lot of money, and if we did a little, we should make less. That's a wonderful formula, and easy to implement if you are working out of

RIGHT: With air conditioning hard to come by, we just stuck our 20-foot legs out the window to stay cool. Coincidentally, passersby and customers found it pretty cool as well.

Six months in business and the production moved to a narrow townhouse on West 56th Street.

your apartment, designing and selling the product yourself. Now, the wake and work routine was over: I would leave my apartment every day for the sixth floor of a townhouse at 29 West 56th Street. It was a small space with an elevator, but it was conveniently close to the shoe industry. Not close enough, however, for us to feel confident that the customers would necessarily find us during the next Shoe Show. That became our next challenge: with no publicity budget to speak of, how could we let the industry know we were there?

With the timely gift of a few pairs of shoes for the neighbors, we were able to hang a twenty-foot banner across the street, which read, "Act I, Scene II." It was legible from at least three blocks east or west. Unsure if our application for a permit for the banner would fly, we found out that the inspector who ruled on such matters didn't work on weekends. So the banners went up Friday and came down on Monday—which, conveniently, was when the Shoe Show took place.

Under the pretense of window washing, we gained permits from the buildings department and suspended scaffolding from the roof of the building. We enlisted brave models with more ambition than inhibition, who were willing to parade outside our sixth-story windows. We hired a small truck and a cameraman who focused up at the scaffolding. The combined effect—banner, scaffolding, models, and cameraman—drew the attention of hordes of pedestrians, including the buyers, who, having found us, wedged their way into the small elevator and the not much bigger showroom. Over the next two years the buyers did come, and the shoes did sell, and all the while we conjured up ways to outdo our last production.

I knew that if I allowed us to settle for being just a shoe company, we might go the way of companies like Penn Central.[9] The business could never be just about the shoes we sold—they would change every few months. It needed to be about the lifestyle the shoes represented, and to stand for something that would survive the unpredictable winds of fashion. The best bet, oddly enough, was unpredictability itself. At one point, mannequins became the prop *du jour*, showing up on the elevator and in the hallway, dressed as buyers in the showroom, clutching a pad and pencil. At our next show, a pair of twenty-foot legs with high heels were draped outside our window, piquing the interest and awareness of all. At every turn we made sure the cameras kept rolling . . . and the show went on.

During our first year, we did $5 million in business, and made $1 million in profits. The business grew quickly. Add to that the fact that we had too many people (mostly cigarette smokers) in too tight a space, another move became inevitable. It wasn't long before we left West 56th Street, and eventually settled at 29 West 57th Street. Our growth was exhilarating, and I was bursting with energy. I knew we were on the right track, which was hard enough in this business, and I knew that we needed to continue to grow. But it wasn't only about getting bigger, it had to be about getting better.[10]

While we wanted to grow, we knew we had to stay true to the stores that were already proving to be loyal to us. That was where things became a little more complicated. Early in my career, I worked to create a product with as broad a reach as possible, selling as many shoes as I could to as many people as I knew how. But when our distribution became more exclusive, I quickly realized that, to build a business, it would not be enough just to sell to the customer once. I would have to sell to them again and again: another pair of shoes, a compatible bag,

FOOTNOTE #8
UNA VIDA

Vinny was devoted to KCP, and was a wonderful character. He never married, never took a vacation, and worked and smoked tirelessly for years (dying, very sadly, in January 1997, after being sick for months with non-Hodgkin's lymphoma). He was nothing short of amazing and it was a sad, sad day for everyone at Kenneth Cole Productions when Vinny left us.

FOOTNOTE #9
TIED TO THE TRACKS

People in the city still regret the destruction of the original Penn Station, those huge steel arches that held up one of the city's empires. The Penn Central Corporation would most likely have been the largest in the world today had they just realized what business they were in. They thought they were in the train business. But when cars and buses became cheaper travel options and flying became more convenient, PCC was busy fixing their tracks, instead of adapting to their customers' changing needs. Had PCC realized they were in the transportation business, they wouldn't have disappeared along with their trains.

LESSON: *As I wander through the trees, I learned I'd better not lose sight of the rest of the forest.*

"Our bags also come in camel."
—Kenneth Cole

FOOTNOTE #10
GROW OR DIE

Once, when my oldest daughter, Emily, was just four, we had her cousins over—all boys. As boys do, they ripped through the house, terrorizing everyone and leaving little paths of destruction in their wake.

That night, when I was tucking Emily into bed, I said, "Em, your mother and I think you are perfect. Just perfect. In fact, so much so that we want to keep you exactly the way you are. So, starting tomorrow, we're not going to be feeding you anymore."

Emily looked alarmed. "But if you don't feed me, I'll starve."

Even at four, Emily knew she couldn't always take me seriously. Still, the simple truth of what she said that night comes back to me often. Shortly after, we had a company-wide sales meeting. The **THEME** *In business, as in life, you either grow or die.*

or the latest leather coat. Our few customers were our lifeline, and they were getting to know us through our brand, and this needed our undivided attention and would demand our unwavering focus from conception to consumption.

In essence, I'd come to realize, if nothing else, a brand provides customers with a strategy. When you walk into a store, you see something you like. The first thing you're likely to do is test it. You might pull it off the rack, check the price, and check the label. If it passes those tests, you'll take it in to the dressing room and test the fit in front of the mirror. Hopefully you will see something, *someone* you like. Maybe you'll see the new you, or the competent you, or the on-a-yacht-sailing-around-the-world you. At best you will get a glimpse of who you want to be. At worst, you'll see who you're glad you're not.

Choosing what works is often a difficult process, and brands can help you navigate the multitudes of options. No one has unlimited time and patience, and a brand can simplify any shopping experience. The brand is the common denominator that should make certain lifestyle decisions easier.

To take a brand that is positioned in only the coolest stores and expand its distribution calls two aspects of the business into question: since the product would have to go to less exclusive stores, its price would probably have to change; and for that to happen, we would have to secure different sources of production; and that would risk compromising its integrity and quality. I was already catering to my ideal client, and changing the integrity of the brand seemed like a good way to lose everything that had brought me to this dilemma in the first place. Instead, we inverted the equation, and rather than look to sell the same product to more customers, we sought to sell *additional* products to the *same* customers— along with their friends and companions.

The birth of the men's shoe line in 1984 was our first leap in this direction. Suddenly, we were making shoes for the companions of our female customers—those with similar interests, lifestyles, and aesthetics, but different hormones. Designing a men's line of shoes, I soon realized, was an extremely intuitive and personal process. Essentially, I was designing shoes for myself. To design any product you have to put yourself in the customer's proverbial shoes, and to do this, you must get to know them intimately: what they like, what they see, what they read, where they go. Well, I had met the customer, and he was I.[11]

Our decision to launch the men's line of shoes coincided with a new trend. Unlike in previous times, when men owned one pair of black shoes and one pair of brown, both of which they resoled every year or so, a growing number of men were discovering that it was okay to have more. There was a new consumer in the market, a guy who went shopping not every year, but every week, and would buy more shoes than six-packs.

As the company evolved with this customer, we needed to control what our brand was becoming in the process, and for that we needed to open a store of our own, to showcase the product in the way we wanted. We could no longer rely solely on multi-brand distribution and specialty stores like

THERE'S NO BUSINESS LIKE SHOE BUSINESS. An early home production.

FOOTNOTE #11
IT'S ONLY FITTING

With the introduction of menswear in 1997, our company presented its first runway show (I was still young and naïve; now I'm less young, but still naïve). Typically, these shows feature fifty to seventy-two looks, shown on twenty-two to twenty-seven models. So for our first event we worked months of eighteen-hour days, all to prepare for what would ultimately be a twenty-minute show. It was an obscene amount of time, money, and resources but this was our first presentation to the press and to customers. The day before the show, when everyone was running around, I had to decide what to wear and, looking around quickly, pointed to a particular outift and said, "That one will be fine." I was told, "No, no, you're the designer, you can't wear that!" But to the contrary, maybe what makes this all so personal is that I *do* wear it.

LESSON: *Take care of others, but don't forget to suit yourself.*

FOOTNOTE #12
CANDIE'S LITTLE GIRL

Candie's was later bought back by my brother Neil, who, having left the nest just a few years after I did, runs it successfully today. He had started a company called No Excuses (now called Candie's, Inc.) that made women's sportswear and various other accessories. Today they manufacture and sell Candie's and Bongo footwear, jeans, and accessories.

LESSON: *We are all connected through our jeans.*

Bergdorf's and Bloomingdale's, two of the best. We needed the ability to tell our story in our own words, unedited, and we could only do that with our own stores, which needed to be carefully designed and thoughtfully situated so as not to compete with but to reinforce the relationship with our existing customers. So in 1985 our first store opened on the trendy, highly trafficked Columbus Avenue in Manhattan, featuring both men's and women's shoes. That was soon followed by a store on similarly trendy Union Street in San Francisco.

Shortly thereafter I came to realize that the best way to continue to grow was through the addition of an alternative label. The business was changing. Value was taking on a whole new meaning. It became more about functionality, practicality, and longevity than about price. Having had countless purchase regrets, most people had come to realize that, if they paid one dollar for a pair of shoes and never wore them, they had paid too much.

Value came to mean having a product that serves as many lifestyles as possible for the longest amount of time, and it is critical to the growth of the brand. So I began to look for complementary forms of branding.

Our first branding effort outside of Kenneth Cole was "So What?, A Kenneth Cole Production," designed to be a hipper, cheaper alternative. Before "So What?" came to market we were alerted that there was a potential trademark problem, so, in 1984, our new diffusion product was delivered to stores instead as "What's What." Some years later we married it to a sub-brand called Aerosoles, which we sold in 1987 to the company's management.

With the sale of What's What, we simultaneously started a junior brand named Unlisted; that coincided with my family's sale of Candie's, so I was now, for the first time, comfortable

DOES THE MAN MAKE THE SHOES OR DO THE SHOES MAKE THE MAN?

FOOTNOTE #13
THREE FOR ONE AND ONE FOR ALL

At Kenneth Cole Productions, we offer three brands. We need to. The realities of the business environment have become too complex to do business with one brand alone. It's not just that the customers are changing—so are the circumstances in which they make their decisions.

The company's three brands are each different, but yet all related to the umbrella brand. The signature brand, Kenneth Cole, is intended to be contemporary in design, urban and sophisticated, well made and reasonably priced.

Our diffusion brand, Reaction, is younger and more casual, influenced by the motion and energy of the city. Reaction customers update their look often, seeking both innovation and function. In an existence where so much of what we do is about action, how better to respond but with . . . Reaction.

However, there also exists a junior market that is *much* trendier: a broader-based business that speaks to another customer, one who shops more often, looking for more disposable fashion. Despite how responsive and impressionable this customer can be, they prefer to consider themselves otherwise. Hence, Unlisted. Unlisted is a brand designed for hipper (and even younger) customers who change their preferences often, and who shop, not every season, but every day. It's a consumer base much broader than the other two, which has brought a new dynamic into the company.

All three of the brands share, I hope, integrity, quality, and most of all, consistency. All support and serve each other. If the brand isn't consistent throughout all its executions, then it has failed. So if we execute one concept beautifully in shoes, but use a different concept for watches, and yet another for handbags, then we let you, the customer, down. Even if done well, if each execution speaks to a different customer, a different aesthetic, or a different value, we have clouded the brand's expectation. Translation: "You're on your own."

LESSON: *You can't please all the people all the time, but there's no harm in trying.*

offering a competitive junior alternative. [12] Several years later, in 1994, we introduced another diffusion brand, Reaction, hoping to further enable the Kenneth Cole label to remain somewhat exclusive and still maintain its edge.[13]

Other accessories soon followed. Our first effort was to license our brand to a handbag company called The Blum Companies in 1988, a business we would acquire several years later. Paul Blum, one of the company's principals, has been with me since and has been crucial to the growth of Kenneth Cole Productions. In fact, Paul is now its president.

Over the next ten years many other accessories were launched under license with some of the finest companies in their respective businesses. Stepping outside the accessories arena, we faced a big hurdle several years later when we introduced menswear (see p. 84), it significantly evolved our relationship with the customers, a huge step that also transformed the brand, as important and defining as anything we had ever done. It was also a potential launching pad for the womenswear that we hoped would follow. I was intent on accomplishing something I had never even dreamed about only months before: figuring out what women want to wear above the ankles. I knew that men had become tougher to satisfy because they were beginning to reassess their fashion needs every few months. But women were doing it every three minutes, so creating a clothing line for them could clearly be the ultimate test, and an important opportunity to become a full lifestyle brand. We found the best women's wear company (Liz Claiborne) and off we went (although I'm not quite sure where). And in the interest of ultimately tying all this together, we then introduced a product totally alien to everything I had ever worked with: fragrance.[14]

In an effort to keep the company focused, all of our resources have been unified and consolidated. Each brand, while catering to a slightly different customer, attempts to marry good design and high quality. Kenneth Cole, the brand, remains the singular master, with Reaction/Kenneth Cole, and Unlisted, a KC Production, benefiting from its marketing efforts. Ultimately these efforts serve all these initiatives, incorporating a component of the master brand but serving different customers. This is all done in both genders for wholesale, retail, Internet, and catalog distribution.

"Head over heels?"
—Kenneth Cole

It's complicated, and there are many moving parts, but those complications thus far have allowed us to keep growing, without ever compromising brand integrity. (Having personally outgrown a brand once before, with Candie's, I was determined not to do it again.) I had learned that one brand doesn't have to be all things to all people.

KCP has kept expanding, growing at a sales rate of between 22 and 60 percent a year, for twenty years, every year except for 2001 (due to 9/11 and other circumstances), at a compound annual growth rate of nearly 30 percent over that same twenty years. Eighteen years after opening our first store, we have nearly one hundred stores nationwide, carrying a wide range of clothing and accessories. We're in seventeen countries, and design and market seventy-three products between the three labels for both genders, and now for kids as well.

The business has required a huge personal investment. The challenge has been to balance expectations with possibilities, dreams and desires with realities. It has worked some days, and not so well others. And it keeps changing, as I do as well, reimagining who we are and what we are about at every turn.

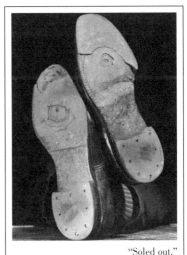

"Soled out."
—Kenneth Cole

FOOTNOTE #14
IT STARTED TO MAKE SCENTS

First, I had to do everything else. Women's shoes, men's shoes, handbags, accessories, outerwear, and then men's and women's clothing took top priority as we expanded our product line and got to know our customers better. Which ended up being a good thing, because with fragrance, we would need to get closer to them than we ever had been before.

From a designer's point of view, however, scent can be as frustrating as it is intriguing. It's intangible—you can't see it or touch it, and it's often defined by the package it comes in. When we decided to do a fragrance, we contacted LVMH/Givenchy, who had been pursuing us for years. When we got back in touch, they were thrilled.

We're ready, I said, let's do this. If we start now, when do you think we'll have the product out on the shelves?

Eighteen months, they said.

I thought they were kidding. I told them I could make two babies in the time they needed to bring one bottle of fragrance to the market. Well, that's the time it takes, they said.

We thought it over. We knew we would want to do both a women's and men's scent eventually, so we decided that we might as well go ahead and do the two at once.

Although initially we were reluctant to do a fragrance at all, eighteen months later, right on time, twins were born. A fragrance for men and a perfume for women were delivered, encased in silver and gold mesh.

So the plan was to take these new fragrances and combine them with a marketing campaign that sought to redefine sensuality—a lofty goal: to talk about not just passion but compassion; not just form but substance; and in terms that were not just sexual but intellectual.

We hired a creative agency to help with the campaign, and photographer Philip-Lorca diCorcia to shoot it. The images of people wearing specific buttons with messages such as:

On Woman: "My body" On Man: "My choice"

On Man (with a photo of a gun): "Safety 1st" On Woman: "Amendment 2nd"

On Man: "Pro-Recycling" "Pro-Diversity" On Woman: "Pro-Phylactic"

It didn't have the impact that we had hoped, so we decided to do other ads in-house. The result was what people had grown to expect from us, and a tag line we just couldn't resist.

"Just what the world needs," it read. "More of our two scents."

STIR THE AIR.
-KENNETH COLE

THE NEW FRAGRANCES FOR MEN AND WOMEN

1986 WHILE THE WORLD'S MEDIA OBSESSED OVER THE NUMBER OF SHOES A FRIENDLY DICTATOR'S WIFE OWNED, WE HAD A SLIGHTLY DIFFERENT CONCERN.

"Imelda Marcos bought 2,700 pairs of shoes.

She could've at least had the courtesy to buy a pair of ours."

—Kenneth Cole

New York
353 Columbus Ave.

San Francisco
2078 Union St.

1987
WE DIDN'T KNOW HOW TO CURE AIDS, BUT WE KNEW HOW TO CONTAIN IT.
SLIGHT PROBLEM—IT WAS ILLEGAL TO ADVERTISE CONDOMS.
...NOTHING VENTURED, NOTHING GAINED.

"Our shoes aren't the only thing we encourage you to wear."
—Kenneth Cole

This public service message is paid for by Kenneth Cole in conjunction with
the American Foundation for AIDS Research.

1990 REDUCE, REUSE, RECYCLE. ALL IN ONE AD.

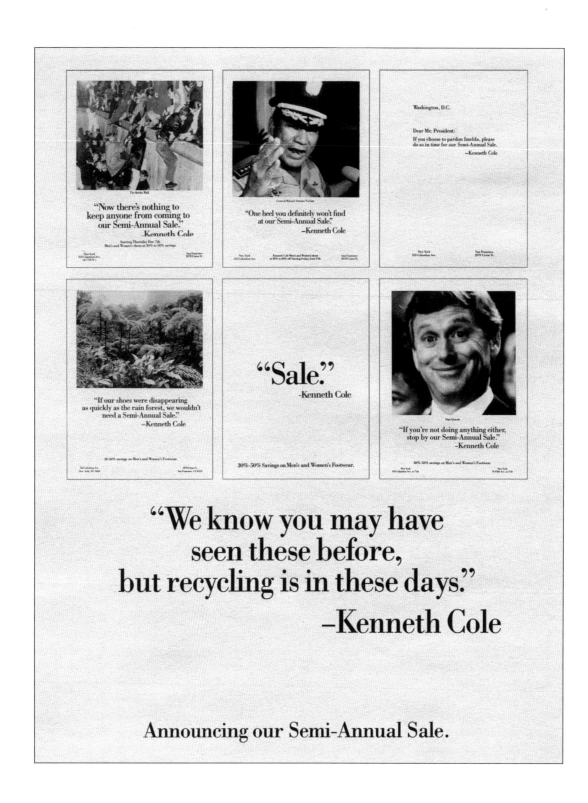

four

TAKE A STAND
OR STEP ASIDE

I emphatically pursue opportunities to communicate important social messages and, less often, political perspectives. Maybe it was the influence of my dynamic and persevering father, or my mother, always encouraging and supportive, or my grandfather—or for that matter John F. Kennedy, or maybe Nelson Mandela.   Perhaps it's divine insistence, or a demented belief in the power of change. For whatever reason, I've never been reticent to take a stand about my beliefs and opinions.

As a dentist, my grandfather held ardent beliefs about certain health issues, and he wasn't quiet about them. "You are what you eat," he always told me, forty years before that saying became part of America's health mantra. At times, he was outspoken to the point of being a public menace. Long before the rest of the world, he promoted his conviction that smoking was detrimental to everyone exposed. When people lit up in his presence, regardless of where we were, he asked them to put out their cigarette. Once, when I was eight, we stepped into an elevator with someone who was smoking. My grandfather asked him nicely to extinguish his cigarette, and when the man refused, my grandfather put it out for him. Now I'm not as gutsy or fanatical as he was, but to this day I am inspired by his passion.

I also track my course back to 1963. I didn't experience the same horror and shock the adults around me did when President Kennedy was assassinated. In fact, I don't know that I was totally clear on what the President even did. I was certainly too young to understand all the implications of that day. But by watching the grief and the panic of the adults around me, I did understand that something had

RIGHT: 1994 ad in the *Washington Post* illustrating the bi-partisan person I am.

"If you insist upon the right wing, we'd like to make a suggestion."

-Kenneth Cole

President Nelson Mandela

"A nation of people improved
their standing overnight.
All without a Semi-Annual Sale."

–Kenneth Cole

30-60% Off

Starting Thursday, June 9th, save on selected Kenneth Cole merchandise at our Semi-Annual Sale.

95 Fifth Ave.(at 17th St.) NYC, NY 10003   353 Columbus Ave. (at 77th St.) NYC, NY 10024

changed, probably in the same way that my children will remember that something changed after 9/11. I was aware that something much larger than what happened in my day was going on out in the world. And if nothing else, it made me want to know exactly who this President guy was, and what he did that was so important.

By the time I was in college, I was a political science major, fascinated by the process of representative government, and aiming toward a degree in law. And while my life has in some ways veered from that direction, in other ways, it has followed a parallel path.[16]

A designer is a dreamer; a visionary who sees not only what is there, but what is not, and deals with reality as well as fantasy. Since perception often precedes reality, we often think that if we can make things appear a certain way, it will become our reality. I guess we would like to think a public servant is, or could be, like a designer, working to create an ideal society, where justice and virtue are viewed as personal responsibilities as well as public expectations that transcend personal style.

In fact, politicians and designers are in some ways very much alike. Designers are usually the creators and/or spokespeople for a brand from which they're often indistinguishable. By the same token, a politician is known for his platform. Both designer and politician have to establish a relationship with their audience; both are marketed; both are vulnerable to shifting public opinion. Just as a designer needs to establish who he is to his customer, so does a politician. Whereas a designer uses company-funded marketing to communicate his message, and a politician uses campaign-financed advertising, both require the attention of the free press. And they both benefit most of all from customer satisfaction and word of mouth.

We have witnessed how watchful that media eye can be, and how gluttonous. The mainstream media in America is insatiable when it comes to digging up dirt on public figures and politicians, and over-sensationalizing issues we know are not relevant. Wars, hunger, and the environment are too often cast aside for speculations on a starlet's kleptomania, a congressman's extramarital affairs, or a socialite's temper tantrums. Heroes are manufactured quickly and destroyed even more quickly.

This is purely the result of business interests. When the press creates icons, they sell newspapers, magazines, and TV shows; and when they destroy those same icons, they sell even more. Thus the media guarantees itself a constant flow of business.

The effect of this process on our psyche and our politics is profound. We've created a system that encourages the media to scrutinize to the point of terrorizing candidates, creating standards for our politicians that few private citizens uphold. As a result, many of our brightest, most qualified people are reluctant to come forward to lead.

FOOTNOTE #15
MOTHER SHIP

Due to a sibling's medical struggle in childhood, my mother, Gladys Cole Levine, often journeyed to a clinic in Boston. At that time (in the 1970s), she, along with others, took the initiative to create a children's medical center in New York. Up until that time, New York was the only major city in the United States without a pediatric hospital. The clinic later became affiliated with Long Island Jewish Hospital. Her perseverance and dedication to the cause became a sustaining force. She's a powerhouse of energy and resolve to this day.

LESSON: *No matter how much one does, it's all relative.*

FOOTNOTE #16
THERE'S LOGIC IN EVERYTHING

Reflecting back, having gone from law school to a career in design might have seemed like a leap—but the law is a systematic, logical process, and in many ways, so is fashion. Law is "by the book," and the better a lawyer is at mastering and applying what's in the book, the further he or she will go. But there is no book in the business of fashion. You write your own as you go, and the further it is from what's already been written, the better you're likely to do.

THE LESSON? *The only law in fashion is that there are none.*

I have found my own approach of dealing with this phenomenon: humor, which helps us to realize that *we* created this monster, and *we* continue to feed it. By laughing at ourselves, humor can bring a voice of reason into the debate—so I use it whenever I can.

When the wife of Philippine dictator Ferdinand Marcos was exposed as a shoe fetishist in 1986, for example, we retorted with:

"Imelda Marcos bought 2,700 pairs of shoes. She could've at least had the courtesy to buy a pair of ours." (See p. 50)

This was part of an ad series we did over several years with Kirshenbaum and Bond, before eventually taking all our advertising in-house (about 1993) and doing it ourselves.

We also paid tribute to an extraordinary moment in history. When Nelson Mandela single-handedly proclaimed a newly democratic government of South Africa in a bloodless transfer of power after being incarcerated for twenty-seven years, we ran an ad featuring his face with the caption:

"A nation of people improved their standing overnight. All without a Semi-Annual Sale."

We never imagined anyone would have a problem with this, but nonetheless, letters came. We were accused of not being reverential enough and, on top of that, wrong (the transfer of power didn't exactly happen overnight).

When Vice President Dan Quayle was corrected by a Trenton sixth-grader for adding an "e" onto "potato" during a spelling bee, we knew drastic measures were called for. As the press was discussing the VP's lack of initiative, our 1992 tag line, under a picture of the smiling Vice President read:

"Don't forget to vot."

A later ad, using the same Quayle picture, played simultaneously with the opening of our San Francisco Market Street store and read:

Dan Quayle

"Don't forget to vot."
—Kenneth Cole

1992 A POSTER FOR THE OPENING OF A NEW STORE APPEARED . . . THEN DIDN'T?

2001

SOME PEOPLE GET RIGHT TO THE POINT AND OTHERS BEAT AROUND THE BUSH.

1988

Michael Dukakis

George Bush

"Good luck, and may the only loafers we see in the White House be ours." –Kenneth Cole

New York
353 Columbus Ave.

Kenneth Cole shoes are also available
at selected Department and Specialty stores.

San Francisco
2078 Union St.

"If you're not doing anything either, stop by for our grand opening."

Here we ran into a problem. The Quayle posters carrying the ad were so popular that they were all stolen within a day of opening, taken home to grace people's mantels—or dartboards. So much for leaving a lasting impression.

In 1993, one of our ads referred to Hillary Clinton's effort to reform the national health care system (noble and sincere though it was):

"A National Plan to Provide Heeling for All—Why Didn't We Think of That?"

While most of the coverage around both these political figures was loaded, we sought lighter ways to reference the issues without being confrontational.

"A national plan to provide heeling for all.
Why didn't we think of that?"
—Kenneth Cole

Call 1-800 KEN COLE

A few years later, during the race for governor of New York, I made a decidedly different move. The process of running for office breeds two distinct types of politicians: those who say what will get them elected, and those who say what stays true to their brand. The former justify their approach by saying that if what they eventually do is right, their ends have justified their means. It's the "Read My Lips" School of Politics—say what you have to say so you can do what you want to do. The second type of politician believes that his responsibility is not just to tell the community what they want to hear. They offer full disclosure, so that you know what you're buying when you get the product: it's truth in advertising. They seek to remain true to themselves and to their brand.

Mario Cuomo is the second kind of politician. Nowhere was that more evident than in the election of 1994 for a fourth term, when I watched his campaign against George Pataki. Being on both the inside and outside of the political race, I watched as Pataki came along, saying what he

"Next time you hear George Pataki speak,
might we suggest the appropriate footwear."
-Kenneth Cole

Stop by Kenneth Cole on Election Day and receive 20% off our men's or women's rainboots.

95 Fifth Ave. (at 17th St.)   353 Columbus Ave. (at 77th St.)
THE NEW YORK TIMES MAGAZINE / NOVEMBER 6, 1994

FOOTNOTE #17
THE FAMILY BUSINESS

When Maria Cuomo and I were first together, we often went up to Albany to spend time with her family, and invariably discussed the family business—politics. It was fantastic—everyone would passionately debate a woman's right to choose, the death penalty, and other crucial issues in the life of our community. Although the decibel level may have risen, in the middle of it all, I would be pondering my own individual business dilemmas, namely the height of heels and the length of hems (crucial issues if you're a foot or a skirt, or a designer of either). The experience, while a little intimidating, helped me keep my own world in perspective. *I've come to learn that the best time to debate family members is when they have food in their mouths.*

FOOTNOTE #18
THE PARTS ARE
THE SUM OF THE WHOLE

An example of where my principles cross over into traditionally Republican territory: I think that businesses are best served through a fair-market economy with free trade, and that tort reform is an important priority. I also believe that, while individual worker's rights are important, the needs of the employer must always be accounted for; without the company, after all, there would be no jobs. We need to be as concerned about the body as its parts.

LESSON: *Why go to only one party if you can go to two?*

thought he had to say regardless of its validity, so he could one day do what he wanted to do. I witnessed all the distortions and inaccuracies in that race, and became aware of just how little they had to do with my father in-law's record or his vision for the state, which I was privy to, having spent long nights around the table in Albany deep in discussion.[17]

I decided to post the first partisan political ad of my career; however, I knew I couldn't tell my father-in-law about it or he would have told me not to run it. Campaign finance laws required that it not be a business endeavor, so I paid personally to put up a billboard on the West Side Highway, and an ad in the *New York Times*, featuring a mud boot, with the words:

"Next time you hear George Pataki speak, might we suggest the appropriate footwear."

As a man getting his first inside taste of the political system, I wanted to address the growing gap between reality and perception. Was the ad appropriate and responsible? I admit I was compelled at the time more by emotion than by intellect. In my business and in politics, it seemed to me that perception often anticipates reality—and that sometimes reality has little to do with it. If something doesn't look right, they are not likely to embrace it. Hence my decision.

As it turned out, the ad was not a good business decision. Most New Yorkers obviously disagreed with me since George Pataki won the election. There was a certain amount of backlash, and I took it in as part of the process. To me, the ad didn't feel political so much as it felt appropriate. Hence, no regrets. I guess showing the ad and telling this story again isn't much smarter today: George Pataki is now serving his third term.

In 2001 we ran another political ad that, despite our best intentions, delivered its message at exactly the wrong moment. Having witnessed the uncertain presidential election a few months earlier, we wanted to express a concern about the electoral process. The world's greatest

2000 WE HOPED TO HELP PUT VOTING BACK IN FASHION WITH THIS INVITATION TO OUR RUNWAY SHOW, COMPLETE WITH NEW YORK STATE VOTER REGISTRATION CARD AND NO. 2 PENCIL.

democracy had, for only the second time in history, put someone into office who hadn't won the majority of votes. So we shot an ad in the suburbs, where models posed on the curb at the intersection of Bush Avenue and Cheney Lane, next to a sign that read "Dead End." (See pp. 60–61)

It provoked a negative response as soon as it ran in the national press. The ad was perceived by many as anti-Republican, but in fact it was intended to express our frustration, partly about the specific individuals but more about the process. My own political ideology is more independent than strictly partisan, and I am not slavishly aligned with either party.[18]

The perception of our ad as anti-Republican was not the only problem. When we released the ads in late August of 2001, we had no idea what was about to unfold in the coming weeks, and, of course, timing is everything. While our ad may have been considered clever to some on September 10 that year, public perception about almost everything was altered the next day. The nation understandably did not have room for that kind of dialogue, and would not for months afterward. Every American understood the immediate need for solidarity. Before that moment, the ad's appropriateness could be debated, but in this new context, it was inappropriate by all standards.

We tried to do as much damage control as we could, pulling the ads from the Texas papers and rerouting them to Nevada, and then after 9/11 pulling them altogether. Despite these efforts, we received a surge of criticism. Agreeing with our critics and feeling that they deserved an honest response, we sent out a letter of apology to all those who wrote in, saying that we understood the inherent responsibility for corporate America to act appropriately and differentiate between what is social and what is political. We added that we had regretfully crossed the line.

If all companies with an advertising budget voiced their political opinions, it would be chaotic. So, with few exceptions, our corporate agenda is to advocate social responsibility, not partisanship. By and large our ads have been well received, and the response overwhelmingly supportive.

I guess because of our message and advertising themes, and considering my personal relationships, I am often asked if I have any political ambitions of my own. I don't. With little governmental oversight, no timetable but my own, few restrictions, and no one to report to (other than shareholders, in my case, and, more importantly, my family), I, and others in my position, can be more effective public servants by remaining in the private sector. And the truth is that, with the will and the right resources, private individuals can do so much for our communities. The resources at my disposal are extraordinary, and as long as I focus them thoughtfully, I think I can serve a constituency or community as well as many politicians can. And that puts me right where I want to be—with the ability to put my best foot forward, while trying to keep the other one out of my mouth.

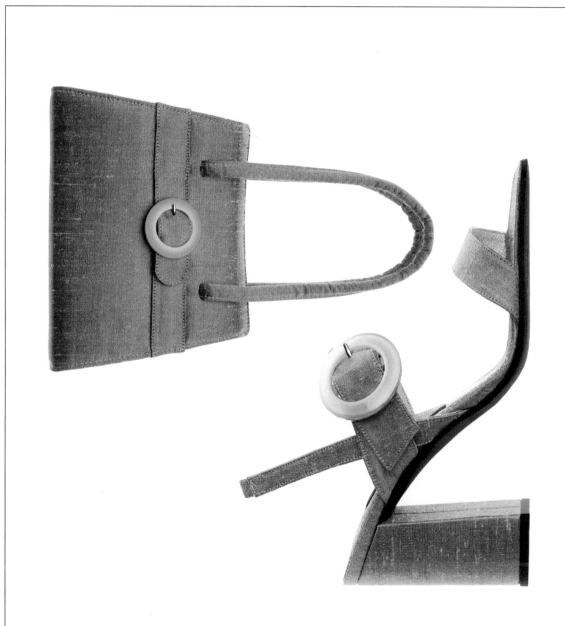

"We had hoped this ad would change the world,
but we blue it."

—Kenneth Cole

five

MIND YOUR OWN BUSINESS

As soon as I saw the headlines in the *New York Times* that Sunday morning in 1992, my heart sank. Changes in the industry brought on by a massive economic downturn already had me feeling uneasy. As a wholesaler, I never wanted a single retailer to represent too large a percentage of my business, but with the consolidations, collapses, and takeovers of the early 1990s, that was becoming impossible to avoid. Many department stores had folded, and most of those that were left were highly leveraged and in debt. Federated, one of our largest customers, was acquired by Campeau in 1988 and in bankruptcy a year later. Macy's, another important customer, had recently acquired one third of Federated's assets, which enabled the Campeau acquisition, and now they, too, were in bankruptcy. Then the Sunday paper arrived bearing the headline: "Federated in Hostile Move to Take Over Macy's."

This was devastating news. In one headline, my position, in my mind, had gone from uncomfortable to precarious. Of the original forty or so department stores with which we had done business, only about fifteen remained, and all were struggling to control their cash flow. They all needed, it appeared, to lower their expenses and generate more profitable sales, which could be accomplished either by selling cheaper, or buying better, or both. Selling cheaper wasn't really an option. This was a time in America when stores were already understaffed, and you couldn't find a salesperson on the floor. Therefore, the only option was to buy cheaper. More than likely, this would mean getting product straight from the factory and cutting out the middleman whenever possible.

RIGHT: Post black Monday, October 1987.

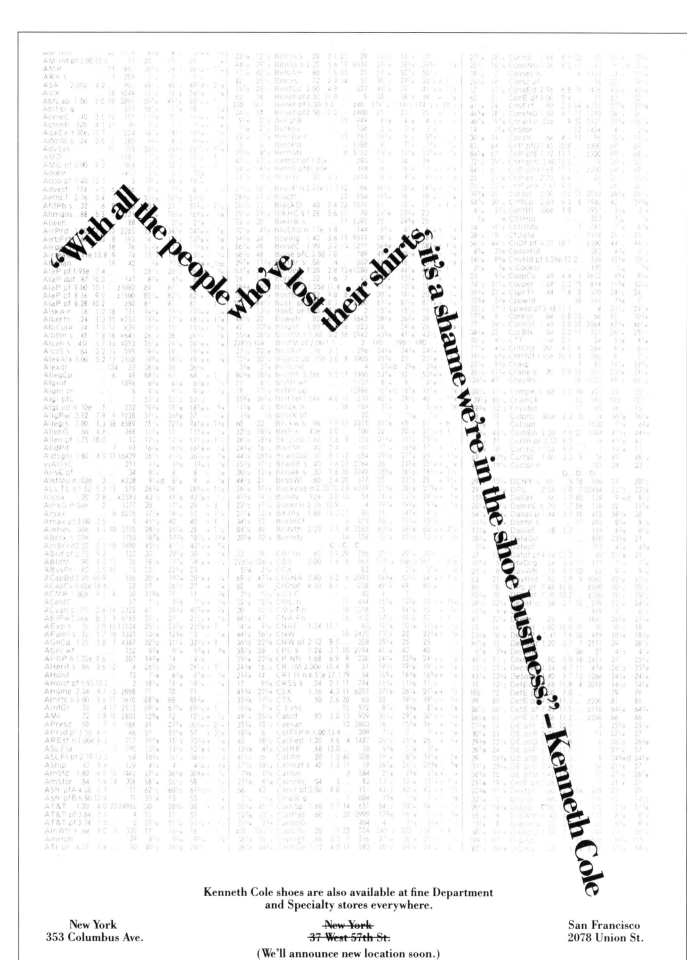

69

"Ready for fall?"
—Kenneth Cole

"These are the times to try men's soles"
—Kenneth Cole

I realized at that moment that I was the middleman. This was a very unsettling moment, as business was already tough. When things are good, people traditionally want to do more of what's working. Only when things are tough do they consider creative alternatives, but that's how we have always positioned ourselves. As a result, in tough times we have always done well, and in good times, we have, for the most part, done even better. Still, I feared the worst; that my career would become a relic, like the black and white television repairman, the eight-track cassette distributor, and the rotary telephone salesman.

But by the next morning, I realized I was wrong. It was true that business was tough, margins were difficult, and there was no room for middlemen, but the assumption that had led me down the road of assured failure was that I was the middleman. I realized, after a full night of not sleeping, that I didn't have to be.

Because conceivably a customer could walk into Macy's or Bloomingdale's looking for a pair of Kenneth Cole shoes, and then walk out if they didn't find them. If I grew my relationship with the customer successfully, Kenneth Cole—the brand—would become the customers' *destination* at the big stores, adding value to our business, to the department stores that hosted us, and, ultimately, to the customer's style. In essence, the retailer would become the middleman, albeit a necessary one.

In order to build that relationship and establish a larger presence, we needed a definitive and consistent point of view. We would need to open more of our own stores in markets where the customers didn't know us. Opening our own stores would enable us to reach the customer who wanted an alternative to department stores, while retaining control over how our product was presented. Through our own retail stores, I could make sure that Kenneth Cole made a unique, distinct, and lasting impression that would also translate in department and specialty stores. There was just one hitch: retail was going to require much more capital than the business had needed up to that point. And as a cautious businessman, I wasn't comfortable leveraging all I had worked for. Instead, I began to rethink my entire business strategy. It was time to consider alternatives, including, if necessary, going public to bring in outside capital.

Since we were a relatively small company at the time, the premier banking firms would not likely be interested in our business; since the costs of taking a small company and a big company public are much the same, they had less incentive to deal with us. However, I believed that much of our success had come from exploring avenues others might not have taken. I convinced myself that at the very least, if I got creative with our business strategy, I would be smarter about the process. I met with several investment bankers, and presented a compelling case for taking Kenneth Cole Productions public. I told them that unlike many of the other offerings, we were a young, growing brand that their customers would relate to. We had created a relatively low-risk fashion business, and made the case that this was not an oxymoron. I illustrated the remarkable rise of our business, and pointed out our vast potential so effectively that I had even convinced myself. Unfortunately, one by one, they told me that we were too small to consider taking public, but that they would be happy to help us explore alternative options, such as selling the company.

I even considered selling Kenneth Cole Productions, and met with potential buyers. But I just couldn't imagine what I would do every day: my work was too much a part of my being, and by this time I couldn't see myself not running the company. But on another level I could envision, as an entrepreneur, the company's bright future almost as clearly as a physical destination. I just hadn't yet found the path.

Two years later, in February 1994, I watched with keen interest as Merrill Lynch took a competitor of mine public. Nine West was about five to ten times larger than Kenneth Cole Productions was, but similarly structured. Merrill Lynch led the deal; Lehman Brothers, who had the industry's top analyst, was the co-lead. The results were spectacular. Nine West surpassed everyone's expectations, and the venture appeared to be extremely lucrative for both

It was this or a well deserved time-out to announce our introduction into kids' footwear.

"Getting by in this business is no small feet.

Or is it?"

-Kenneth Cole

Introducing Children's Footwear

New Jersey • Peterstown B   Las Vegas • Booth #2059

"Going out with the wrong accessories can be a pain in your Aspen."

-Kenneth Cole

101 South Mill Street, on the corner of Main. (970) 920-6875
men's and women's shoes, accessories and leather goods

"What's an ice girl to do in a place like Aspen?"
-Kenneth Cole

(Shop for cool accessories?)

101 South Mill Street, on the corner of Main. (970) 920-6875
men's and women's shoes, accessories and leather goods

Merrill Lynch and Lehman Brothers. That was great news for me. I had a successful business model to follow, and a fine example to point out to bankers. I began to call them again.

Initially, the results were discouraging. Goldman Sachs said absolutely not, and Morgan Stanley also said they were not interested, but when I asked them to reconsider, they said they would, probably just to get me off the phone. Merrill Lynch was somewhat more encouraging. They said they would think it over and get back to me. I was hopeful until one week later, when Mark, their managing director, telephoned.

"We thought about it, Ken," he told me. "But for reasons I can't go into, we just can't do the deal."

Before I could think, I found myself saying, "Well, that's okay, Mark, I think Morgan is going to take us on anyway. But I have to tell you, I think this would be great for Merrill—even better for you than it will be for Kenneth Cole Productions. I believe we've got a brand that your salespeople could relate to. You really should think it over."

Mark was silent. "If we do it," he finally asked, "can we get the lead over Morgan?"

"If I hear back from you by the end of the day," I said. I hung up the phone and sat at my desk, trying not to think what would happen if Merrill Lynch passed.

Later that day, Mark called back.

"Kenneth, if we can have the lead, we'd like to do this offering."

I almost couldn't believe it. I don't think they had ever done a public offering this small. At the time we were a $60 million business, going on $80 million, looking to sell about 20 percent of our stock, of which they would only get a few percentage points. But, boy, what credibility this would give us.

I called Lehman Brothers. I told them I would like them to be the co-lead banker with Merrill Lynch, as long as they gave us the analyst coverage we wanted. They quickly accepted. I guess they believed that Merrill Lynch must be on to something. Some months later, our relatively small company was taken public by two of Wall Street's giants and offered a place on the New York Stock Exchange. Stan Mayer, my executive vice president of finance, and Paul Blum, then vice president of sales and marketing, were vital to the success of this difficult process, as well as a friend, Dennis Kelly, who advised us along the way. We were all ecstatic but anxious—we knew the real work still lay ahead.

"Why *are* you guys doing this?" I finally asked Mark at the closing.

"Because we think you're going to be a $250 million business someday," Mark told me. "That means we're going to get a lot of banking business from you."

I nodded, and laughed to myself. Until this point I was still designing every men's and women's collection in small, remote factories in Tuscany and Spain. I had had no plans of ever becoming that much larger. I just wasn't thinking that way. Up until that point, it had never been about being big.

The fact is, we well surpassed those numbers in a shorter time than anyone could have predicted. We grew from a $60 million company to a $250 million company over the next few years, and by 2001, with licences sales, exceeded $1 billion in retail dollars. Now, having secured better, worldwide sourcing, and having our own retail, licensing, and wholesale business, we had created a vertical model that ensured we would never again be the middleman.

We have other concerns now, and we have to handle them as a public company. But no matter what challenge we face, I find myself reflecting upon the power one holds just by changing perspective. I guess if one can become a production company in the course of an hour and a half, one can find their way out of the middle in whatever time necessary. And with openness and the necessary objectivity to assess our

That's right, Boris, we now have two stores in Boston."
—Kenneth Cole

FOOTNOTE #19

THE WORST MAY NOT BE SO BAD

Six months prior to the opening of our new flagship store in Rockefeller Center, we approached our new neighbor, NBC, to see if they would consider covering a runway show in the plaza, as a feature for the *Today* show and its seven million viewers. All the morning shows love fashion, but until then none had ever covered a runway show live.

After a few conversations with the producers and Katie Couric, NBC committed to covering our Fall '01 Runway Show, giving us a spot on the seven o'clock and eight o'clock segments and more on the nine o'clock segments. We in turn agreed to construct a clear tent in Rockefeller Center that would likely cost close to a million dollars.

It was an extraordinary commitment on our part, and knowing how unpredictable news can be, we wanted some assurance that they would not back out on their part, even if there was *breaking news.*

"Worst-case scenario," they said to us, "if there's breaking news, you'll get bumped from the eight o'clock segment. But you'll definitely be on the nine o'clock segment."

The week before there had been news of two shark attacks in Florida, and every paper and news program was talking about them. "What if it's something as serious as a shark attack on Jones Beach?" I asked the producers. "Are you still going to cover us?"

"If there's a shark attack, you will probably get bumped from the eight o'clock segment," they told me. "But we'll go ahead with it in the nine o'clock segment."

It was the first day of fashion week: September 10, 2001. Ironically, considering what would happen the next day, the theme for our show was prophetic: anti-violence, promoting gun safety. At nine o'clock that morning, our show ran on schedule in a clear tent. Katie Couric interviewed me live backstage and they shot part of the show live. It aired and was covered in all three segments without incident, to the delight of everyone. To this day, an unprecedented coup.

Twenty-four hours later, I couldn't believe that I had considered a shark attack the worst conceivable thing that could happen in the United States. I felt like we were watching the world fall apart in front of our eyes, and in some ways, we were. There was no coverage of anything but the Twin Towers that day, nor would there be any coverage of anything else for weeks to come. Of course, the rest of fashion week was canceled.

It became so clear that day that one's perspective can change radically within the span of an instant.

LESSON: *I learned that you can never anticipate what will happen; all you can really do is prepare for the worst, if you can even imagine that scenario, and hope for the best.*

SOHO, NEW YORK CITY

AMSTERDAM

circumstances, as entrepreneurs we should be able to continue to find acceptable solutions.

But when I picked up the paper that Sunday morning back in 1992 and saw the impending apocalypse, I felt ill. My intense fears lasted only one day, but one day in deep panic can seem like an eternity to a man with a short attention span. By the next morning, I had a plan. I had a goal and a mission, and even though it would take two more years to convince an investment bank to help us get there, I had caught a glimpse of where we were going. From that point on, I knew it was just a matter of how we were going to get there and how long it would take.

The months that preceded and followed going public involved work overload, with every waking minute spent assessing and reassessing our goals as a company. Guided by the theory that you can be successful in business working only half a day (any twelve hours you choose), I was becoming a stranger to my family. During one of these very hectic periods, my four-year-old daughter Catie came in to my home office and asked me if I would do something with her. I told her it would have to wait for now.

"What are you doing?" she asked me.

"Working," I told her.

"Why do you work so much?" she asked me.

"Because it needs to get done," I told her.

"Well, who gives you the work?"

"I give it to myself."

"Well, aren't you the boss?"

"Yes, but that's why I have to do it. Otherwise it might not get done."

"Oh," she said and walked away.

SOUTH BEACH, MIAMI   ROCKEFELLER CENTER, NEW YORK CITY   SEATTLE

But the next week she came back again, wanting to do something, and again, I was busy.

"Why do you work so much?" she asked again.

"Because no one else will do it."

"But who gives you . . ."

It was the same conversation all over again, and over the next couple of weeks it repeated itself almost to the word as Catie showed up in my home office, again and again. At one point, I told the story to a friend and rabbi, shaking my head.

"I don't understand, she's a bright kid, but clearly she just doesn't get it," I said.

"Well," came his reply, "or maybe *you* don't."

That stopped me. The message was clear—my daughter had needs and I had failed to recognize them. I had often asked myself in those years if I was running the company or it was running me, and suddenly, I had irrefutable proof. I needed to change something if I was going to be a larger part of my home life, and the only way I could do that was to step back, take a deep breath, and empower others.

This was not easy for me, but I knew that for the benefit of the business, as well as my relationship with Catie and the rest of my family, that I needed to learn to delegate—and quickly. So I put into practice one of my favorite mantras: prepare for the worst and hope for the best. Instead of flying off to Europe and Asia ten times a year, I had our European and Asian associates come to us. I hired a great crew of managers, delegated a significant portion of my duties among them, and began working at home on Fridays. I crossed my fingers, held my breath, played with Catie, picked up Amanda at school, and took Emily to ballet.

And the funniest thing happened: business actually improved. By necessity, the business became far more collaborative and strategic. In terms of the well-being of the company, I had clearly made the right

WHEN IN ROME, OR ANYWHERE ELSE FOR THAT MATTER...

LONDON WAS CALLING.
-KENNETH COLE

We're finally coming to New Orleans. Okay bayou?
-Kenneth Cole

OPENING DECEMBER. THE SHOPS AT CANAL PLACE   WWW.KENCOLE.COM   1 800 KENCOLE

"As if Boston really needs more heels from New York."

Kenneth Cole

now open, CHESTNUT HILL • COPLEY PLACE • NEWBURY STREET

www.kencole.com

30781

AK MEDIA

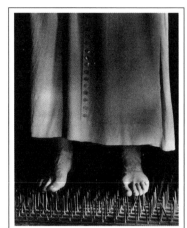

"Spiked heels are not
what they used to be."
—Kenneth Cole

business decision, even though it had been for the wrong reason. I didn't make this move to build the business but to balance it, and it did both.

Which doesn't mean that I worry any less, but that's just my nature. When people ask me what it is about the business that concerns me most, my only honest answer is, everything. What keeps me up at night? All of it.

From the early, hands-on, do-it-all-yourself approach to running a reasonably large business today, I've been in a state of constant transition. When we first went public, I had a brand-new job overnight, and very little idea how I was going to tackle it. I was aware that others in my position didn't often fare very well: of today's Fortune 500 companies, only two have retained their original founders. I also knew that the skills it takes to start a business, to take it from nothing and make it viable, are very different from the skills it takes to operate a large company and to keep investors in a public entity happy. It's a humbling feeling, to suddenly gain that perspective on something that is so innately a part of your being, as much a part of you as an extra limb. In a sharp instant of clarity, I realized that, from an entrepreneurial seed, it had transformed into its own entity, with its own rhythms and cycles, and its own remarkable life.

Entrepreneurs intuitively understand the concept of doing everything that one has to do to get a job done, but no more than called for. They know how to run a business without budgets, or deadlines—and they understand the need to spend what's needed (but not a penny more) to get the necessary results on time. Regardless of what it takes, I am still an entrepreneur, but now my work has different expectations and is geared toward a larger audience. Now, not just the results but also the expectations are assessed in terms that are both quantitative and qualitative.

"Some people don't mind being
seen with the same old bag."
—Kenneth Cole

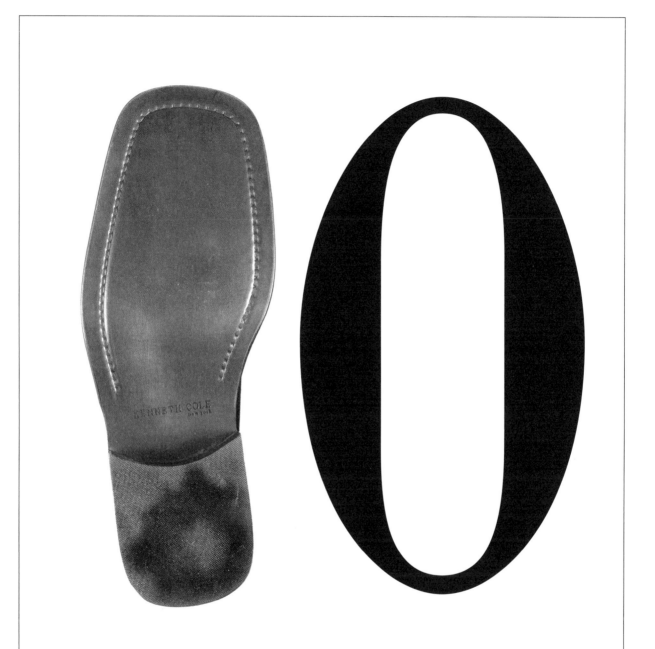

It's our age not our shoe size.
–Kenneth Cole

1996–1998 IF SENSATIONALISM WORKS FOR THE TABLOIDS, WHY NOT CLOTHING AND ACCESSORIES?

The launch of watches with Geneva Watch Company.

The launch of tailored clothing with Hartmarx.

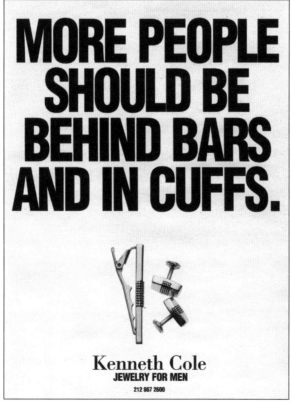

The launch of men's jewelry with Swank.

six

WHY DIS-DRESS?

I must admit that our plans were never as ambitious as the business we have built. Good fortune has showered down upon our company from the start, but the resourcefulness and perseverance of many dedicated associates played the decisive role in our growth. And it just so happens that timely developments in American lifestyle have also helped along the way.

Men's dress, for example, has probably changed more in the last five years than in the prior fifty. We have paid for that stagnation, with interest. Until recently, we all dressed like soldiers in uniform. During the week, that uniform was a gray or navy suit, a white or blue shirt, a tie (usually red), and loafers, black or brown. On weekends, it was torn jeans, T-shirts, and sneakers. Our formal wear was the (identical) black tuxedo, with a (similar) white shirt, and then some (silly) bow tie—en masse we looked like penguins. We regularly showed up at the same costume party wearing the same costume. But that was before the new Internet-inspired generation came of age without ever having worn anything more formal than jeans and sneakers. In a way no one could have expected, everything changed, bringing a hundred-plus-year tradition to a halt with two words—"Casual Fridays"—that implied the type of clothing the average guy did not own, had never worn, and probably did not understand. Men everywhere were traumatized.

What to do? Although the intent was clear, in practice "business casual" would have to be individually interpreted by everyone. For the first time in our lives, men were going to have to develop a personal style. We were being forced to distinguish ourselves by our appearance. Where in the past we had distinguished ourselves by the size of our muscles or our wallets, and how much beer we could drink, the rules were changing. One minute we knew exactly what we were expected to wear, and the next we were called upon to navigate our way in the world of fashion. Neither of the two extremes (very dressy and

RIGHT: The much anticipated introduction of menswear with PDI.

KENNETH COLE
LINKED
TO EXTENSIVE
COVER UP.

KENCOLE.COM

1993 IN THE ABSENCE OF MODELS...

"We considered using models,
but they ended up being an arm and a leg."

- Kenneth Cole

very casual) was going to work. Not on Friday and, shortly afterwards, not during the rest of the week either, not at work, not after, not on weekdays, nor on weekends.

The mission for each and every man was a daunting one, and the toughest part was, no one knew where to go for help, or whom to trust. Their friends and partners didn't necessarily have the best judgment, and salespeople had an agenda. There were few objective sources available. For men, the alternatives were few: quit the job, head for the hills, become a civil servant (where a uniform is provided—nothing like a man in uniform), or find an authority, and for many, that authority was their favorite brand. Brands, after all, should be trustworthy. As long as a brand has been consistent in the past, true to its message, with a distinctive point of view, and didn't let you down, then it has earned your trust.

Now, everyone has made choices they've regretted, and bought things that they never wore except, of course, for those must-have accesories such as clip-on ties, legwarmers, and ascots. First instincts are important, so if a man *thinks* a piece of clothing is right for him, the label serves as confirmation. Although the shopper makes his own decision, the brand often offers guidance. As more and more men needed this kind of guidance, I set out to add value by creating a label they could trust. Civic-minded person that I am, it was the least I could do.

Men were learning to navigate the middle between the overdressed workweek and the underdressed weekend, which was pretty much where our company had always lived. (Nothing like being at the right place at the right time!) We had black leather shoes that looked like loafers but felt like sneakers; we turned briefcases into shoulder bags; and now we made pants and shirts that were sporty enough to be dressed down, yet tailored enough to be taken seriously. We had found two of the finest men's clothing companies in America—Hart, Schaffner & Marx to make our men's tailored clothes, and Paul Davril, Inc. (PDI) the sportswear—and had set out to relieve men everywhere of their onerous burden.

We have tried to evolve with our customers through this perilous new era in which men actually express their personalities through their wardrobe. By offering contemporary fashion solutions, whether needed or not, hopefully bringing a little peace of mind to some.

Strangely, at this same time women were going through the opposite fashion trauma. Whereas men's clothing was overly simplified, womenswear was overly complicated. They had no easy choices. The length of the skirt, the cut of the shirt, the height of the heel—everything was up for grabs. Color, length, silhouette, and how to put it all together were open to interpretation. The options were vast and the results extraordinary. As more women moved into the workplace, the requisite two hours they needed to navigate *all* their fashion options every morning became unmanageable and overwhelming.

Meanwhile, women were also experiencing a fashion miracle of their own. By changing one variable,

65% OF AMERICANS HAVE MORE SUCCESS MAKING THEIR OUTFIT WORK THAN THEIR MARRIAGE

CELEBRATE DIVERSITY.

BURN A TABLOID.

1999 YOU CAN CHANGE AN OUTFIT.

READ THE FOOTNOTES.

CARRY PROTECTION.

HAVE A THEME SONG.

DONATE YOUR TIME.

YOU CAN OUTFIT CHANGE. OR BOTH.

CHOOSE CHOICE.

LAY DOWN YOUR ARMS.

Backstage jitters,
anticipation,
and anxiety; I guess
it's only fitting.

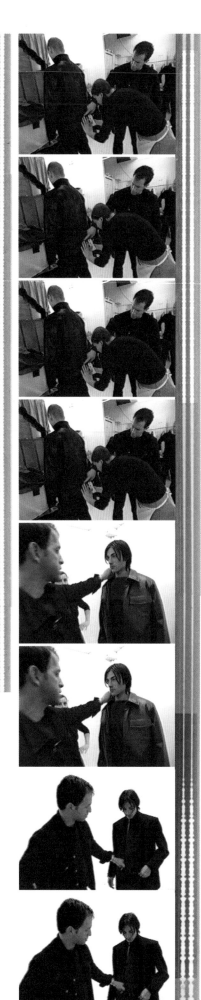

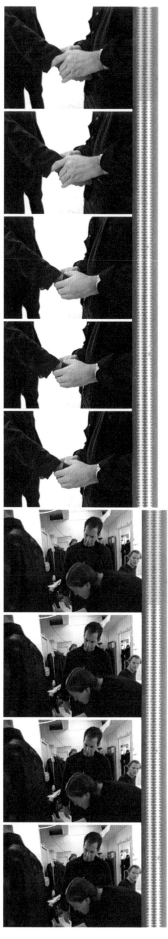

"Be in touch with your sole."
—Kenneth Cole

FOOTNOTE #20
REBEL IN BLACK

Our home experiences the usual incidence of kids asserting themselves contrary to parental guidance; Emily, the oldest, usually leads the fashion charge. I wear my own brand of clothing, and, when I don't forget, I bring home clothes for the family. But, as the girls might tell you, I often neglect to do that. When I do, they look for alternatives. Besides, what teenage girl wants her father choosing her clothes? So sometimes the girls wear other designer's clothes. Which is fine by me, so long as the logos are discreet.

One day, I came home to find Emily wearing a CK (Calvin Klein) logo T-shirt and a smile on her face, ready for a reaction.

I paused for a while, knowing I was being set up, before I finally asked, "Em, what are you wearing?"

"Don't worry, Dad," she said, pointing to her black T-shirt. "I searched far and wide, and finally I found this shirt with *your* initials . . . reversed."

LESSON: *What's important is not always what happens initially.*

women cut their morning prep time from hours to minutes. They also ensured that what they bought would remain fashionable from one season to the next, from day to night. Slimming and timeless, women had discovered their fashion passport: BLACK.

It was no longer just for evening and for fall/winter. It was becoming acceptable for almost anything, anywhere. Fortunately, befitting the compassionate and understanding nature of our company, black was the common denominator of much of what we had provided to our customers over the years. It was appropriate for us, as an urban brand, and now it also worked as a business brand. Black was practical and functional. And if, unfortunately, someone you knew suddenly passed away, you wouldn't have to go home and change.

Black swept the industry like nothing I have ever seen. "The new black," they called it, because black now came in all shades, textures, and silhouettes.[20] Women were now one step closer to easy dressing and still nobody had to look exactly alike, so women didn't suffer the same trauma men had suffered for generations. As we know, Madonna never looked like Morticia Addams, and neither of them resembled a Dominican nun.

The effects of this fundamental shift have been pervasive. Men struggled to define their style and women struggled to define their limits. Guys have come to accept spending more time on what used to be done in an instant, while women have drastically simplified their fashion ritual. Men have sought their personal style by making more choices, and women have happily embraced the simplicity of fewer options. These days, it seems, both are getting dressed in about the same amount of time and feeling more confident in the process.

FOR EVERY DOLLAR
A MAN MAKES
A WOMAN MAKES
75 CENTS.
CHANGE PLEASE

IT'S OUR WAY OR THE RUNWAY

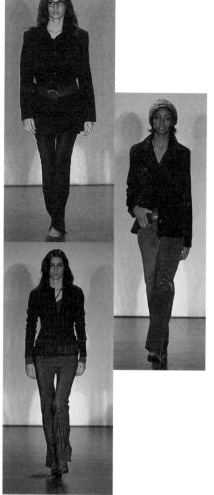

Kenneth Cole

WWW.KC-REACTION.COM

seven

PUT YOURSELF IN MY SHOES

"So you're Kenneth Cole."

When people say that to me, I search their faces to see what that means to them. I need to know if I should smile or duck.

It's dangerous to have your name inside an article of clothing, or even worse, inside a shoe. Shoes, more than anything else one wears, affect not only how you look, but how you feel. In fact, we like to say that there are no such things as bad people—only tight shoes. If you wear a sweater that doesn't fit, you might feel a little silly, and you might even look it. If you wear shoes that don't fit, you could be in pain, and you might be ready to inflict your pain on whoever is causing it, including the guy whose name is emblazoned on the arches.

It has taken me a while to disentangle Kenneth Cole, the man, from Kenneth Cole, the brand. The problem is, when you share your name with a brand, you are often only as good as your product. If the product is cool, you're cool. If the product is innovative, you're a visionary. If the product is in demand, you've got your pulse on the market, you're a fashion hero, and the rewards of praise and patronage are not long in coming. But those rewards are also fleeting. By definition, the terrain of fashion morphs every day.

It's a simple enough truth: people change clothes, and clothes change people. As a response to current events, and a medium for defining exactly what "contemporary" connotes at any given time, fashion reflects who we are, who we want to be, and who we want others to imagine we are. Everything goes

RIGHT: Fall, 1995 catalog.

"Sole searching."
—Kenneth Cole

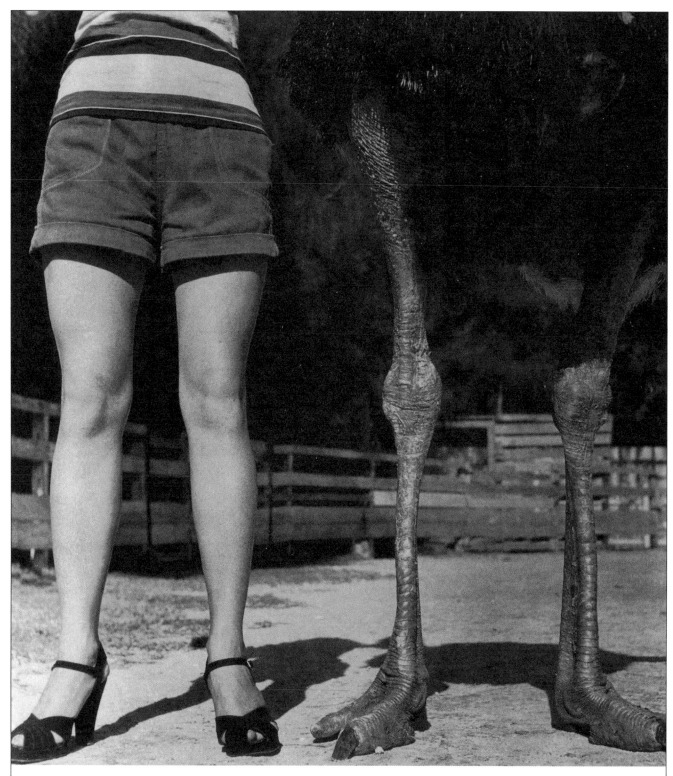

"Not everyone can wear an open toe shoe."
– Kenneth Cole

into that mix: culture, lifestyle, politics, beliefs, and even the weather. Which way the winds are blowing, for example, might determine the length of your hair, the style of your skirt, or the height of your heel.

After all, relativity and perception matter enormously in this world. The only thing that you will be able to count on absolutely is that everything will change. You may have made a great product yesterday, but it means next to nothing if you can't make something equally good today. And great product is very much about timing and perception.

The watchword here: flexibility. It's human instinct to be threatened by change, as we can be pretty stubborn. Old ideas often provide the basis for our decisions—economic, intellectual, or emotional—and even when they don't work out, we often find it hard to abandon them. In business, as in life, it's not easy to be provisional, flexible, and open, and to let go of the outcomes we desire, the products we market. I noticed a long time ago that some people are alarmed by change and others embrace it— they're the ones that usually succeed. Especially in a business where change rules. "Be prepared to abandon ship" might be the motto here. If all else fails, know how to swim. And do get comfortable with the fact that you might be swimming for a while.

It's easier to anticipate change if you are both the creator and the consumer. Conventional wisdom suggests that designers should do their research on the street, to get out there and see what people are wearing, so you know what products are deemed appropriate. My method is different: I tend to look for what it is that people are *not* wearing. And when I get up in the morning and open my closet, and I ask myself what I wish was there. And then I go to work and make it.[21]

When I am in left-brain land, I am consumed by the contemplation of fabrics, belt buckles, and scarf lengths. I become

FOOTNOTE #21
IT'S NOT WHAT'S THERE BUT WHAT ISN'T

There's an old story about two shoe salesmen who are sent to a tropical island to assess the business prospects. They go, they see, they come back home.

"Well, what do you think?" the boss asks the first salesman, who was more experienced.

"There's no business there," he shrugs. "They don't even wear shoes."

The boss turns to the other salesman.

"Not a shoe in sight," observes the younger man. "The possibilities are limitless."

The point being: *It's not always what's there that matters, but often what isn't . . .*

FAMOUS FEET IN ANTICIPATION THAT WE'D ONE DAY BE IN THE SHOE BUSINESS

a tribute to famous feet
Harold Lloyd from the film "Why Worry", 1923
"These are the times to tie men's soles."
-Kenneth Cole
45.

Shoe-ting Stars
Charlie Chaplin, 1920
"An open-toed shoe is a timeless
fashion accessory."
-Kenneth Cole

a tribute to famous feet

Abbott and Costello, 1950

"If What's on second, Shoes on first?"
-Kenneth Cole

a tribute to famous feet

Laurel and Hardy, 1930

"That's another fine mess shoe've gotten us into."
-Kenneth Cole

Shoe-ting Stars

Rudolph Valentino, 1926

"Some accessories are more sheik than others."
-Kenneth Cole

Shoe-ting Stars

Ginger Rogers, 1936

"Ginger's footwork left Fred astare."
-Kenneth Cole

compulsive bordering on manic—I don't know any other way to do it.[22] There are an infinite number of variables to deal with, for example, in the production of shoes, which may be more complicated than any other item in your closet. Even the simplest shoe requires over a hundred steps to manufacture.

Which has brought me, literally, to Italy, sometimes Spain, on occasion Brazil or China, and even, in the past, to Portland, Maine. Precisely because shoes are so complicated, for the most part they have to be designed where they are made, and then sampled. When starting, the last (the mold that is the blueprint for every shoe) comes first, and we take it from there.[23] I'll make a sample, and look at it to figure out how to make it better. Maybe the heel is looking good but the proportion can be better. So I adjust the proportion and make another sample. Now I notice that the lining isn't going to work at all. I make another sample, and another.

But it's not over after that. Even when the last is formed, when the upper is stitched, and when the sole, insole, and heel have finally come together to form a shoe, we still have to grade it: that is, to produce it in nine sizes and two widths. After that we have to produce it in three to five colors and sometimes two materials. Because, in the end, to sell you one pair of shoes, a store should stock no fewer than fifty-four pairs in that given style. Even then, the shoe might not fit, and, if it doesn't, then none of the steps taken to make that shoe will have made a difference.[24]

Those are just some of the aesthetic concerns. Beyond the factory, there is a whole other list of variables to consider, defined by the market. How much will this shoe cost to make, and how much can it sell for? What materials are new, and which are dated? And how are we going to beat the clock to get the product to market before all the above restrictions no

FOOTNOTE #22
I LEFT MY RIGHT BRAIN

The dichotomy between the left and right brain is one that I am comfortable with, and it has manifested itself in the eighteenth-century mahogany partners' desk in my office with drawers on opposite sides. The side facing the door serves my left brain, and contains my files and my computer. The side facing the window and wall accommodates my right brain, and holds my No. 2 pencils and designer's sketch pad. I do believe that, *in a creative business like this, the right can't be left behind, and the left isn't always right.*

FOOTNOTE #23
MAKING IT LAST

There is no such thing as a simple shoe. Satisfying twenty-six bones at one time can get a little tricky, and a sketch on a piece of paper just isn't going to cut it for the pattern maker. Shoes change the minute they take on dimension.

Just getting the last—the basic mold upon which the shoe is built—to work, is an art form in itself. Just as buildings are only as strong as the foundation they rest on, a person is only as strong as the shoes beneath his feet, and the fit and comfort of a shoe is almost totally dependent upon the last it was built upon. The last, then, is the foundation of the foundation. It's the three-dimensional sculpture upon which the rest of the shoe is built. If the last isn't perfect, the shoe is never going to look good or fit well. It's that simple. Is it too pointed? Too arched? Well contoured? Well proportioned? The only way to make a good shoe is to make the last, figure out what's wrong, fix it, and make it again. That translates to patience and a lot of work. Eat only if necessary; sleep optional.

LESSON: *It's not every business where one gets many last chances.*

FOOTNOTE #24
SURVIVAL OF THE FITTEST

A harsh but little known truth about shoes: even the best-fitting shoe is only going to fit about 70 percent of the people that try it on. A reasonably well-fitting shoe may only work for 50 to 60 percent of the people that try it on. Why? Feet are just particular like that, and no two people have exactly the same feet, and sometimes even your own two feet are not the same. No matter what your actual size is, you will not be able to fit comfortably into every shoe in your size. Your feet will always like some shoes better than others, and feel different about them at different times of the day.

LESSON: *Finding something that's right for everyone is a real feet.*

FOOTNOTE #25
WHO, ME?

In 1998, *People* magazine called our office: they wanted to know if I would agree to be named as one of America's "Sexiest People" (specifically, the "Sexiest Businessman" designation) and if I could keep my mouth shut about it until the magazine came out.

My male ego rose swiftly to the occasion. I was ecstatic. But once I settled down and thought through the implications, it became a little more complicated. For years I had been working to reposition our company in an industry often considered trivial and frivolous, making it something that was more meaningful and substantive. There were a lot of adjectives that applied to what we do, but "sexy" wasn't high on the list. On the other hand, what if this was an opportunity to make the marriage of business and ethics sexy by association? (It sounded good, anyway.)

When the magazine came out, my daughters and I had to have a discussion about it. They weren't sure how they felt about the word "sexy" appearing in conjunction with their father, and I couldn't really blame them; after all, I had a few decades on them, and I wasn't sure how I felt about it, either. The younger two had a more nebulous idea of what it might mean, but Emily, the oldest, was a little more cognizant. "Sexy," I explained, is really just another word for "appealing." That was a compliment, and for the most part, that was a good thing.

I guess the **LESSON** *here is that you can fool some of the people, but only some of the time.*

longer apply? That sense of urgency translates into speed to market. Being second to market, although better than being third, undermines everything you have accomplished.

Growing up with my brothers, I remember showing up for dinner at seven if it was called for at seven, and finding it was already half gone. In fashion as in cuisine, the early bird usually eats the best.

Now, if one had none of this to consider, you could create what some people call "true art." You could make shoes for shoes' sake, as it were, or even add a whole other dimension to the universe of fashion, using the most expensive materials, and unlimited amounts of time, and the finest artisans in the world. And if, as well, those shoes were never meant to be worn, but merely to grace a museum shelf, and so didn't need to be comfortable, why, you could make gilded stilts if you wanted to. But for me it is that real-world factor that takes the creative process to a whole different place.

My challenge is to create an extraordinary product within the boundaries that are defined for me. And to do that one has to commit oneself completely to making the newest, finest, most well-fitting and affordable product, and getting it to the market on time. So, if it would make the shoe better, at the last minute we would change the heel, adjust the proportion, and get rid of the laces, and correct the finish. I would go from eighteen-hour days to twenty-hour days, finding some of my best ideas when the conveyor stopped in an empty factory on a quiet night in a little town in Tuscany. I'd work every last second, usually over-caffeinated, going through elaborate steps just to get the sample back in the country, onto the shelf, and in front of the customer on time.

I collect people's reactions to a new style, but most are unable to articulate the reasons behind their response. In all

"Heel."
—Kenneth Cole

"Shoo fly, shoe."
—Kenneth Cole

likelihood, the first thing they'll say is, "I don't like it." Then they might specify: "I don't like that buckle." "I don't like the heel." "I don't like the shoe." Usually they don't specify at all: they just don't buy the shoe. That says enough to me, loud and clear.

We need to be open to input and respond to it, both internally and practically—to listen and to learn. Serving the public's taste certainly beats trying to change it. So the best salesmen aren't the best talkers, they're the best listeners. Day after day I *become* the consumer, registering everything with an open mind and a healthy sense of detachment. I learned early on that my job is not to decide what people should wear, but instead to understand what they want, and give it to them in an unexpected way.

The heel doesn't work? Okay. That kind of a buckle is wrong? Fine. You just don't want it? Then we'd better pay attention. Because actually the customers are telling me exactly what I need to know: what they want. From the time the shoes are in the stores, they are no longer mine, and I am no longer Kenneth Cole, the designer. The businessman, Kenneth Cole, must be able to look at a shoe, or a pair of pants, a leather jacket, or a watch for that matter, and to see it for what it is, and isn't. To make the changes that are suggested by our customers' choices, we keep putting ourselves in their shoes—in the hope that they will keep putting themselves into ours.

Which is not to say that separating the man from the brand has always been easy. I try to leave the designer, businessman, and brand behind at the office, and send home the individual Kenneth Cole before he's too beat-up at the end of the day.**25** Because there, too—there, most of all—the ability to evaluate, transform, and keep changing is crucial to our survival, especially in a house with a wife, three daughters, and a female dog.

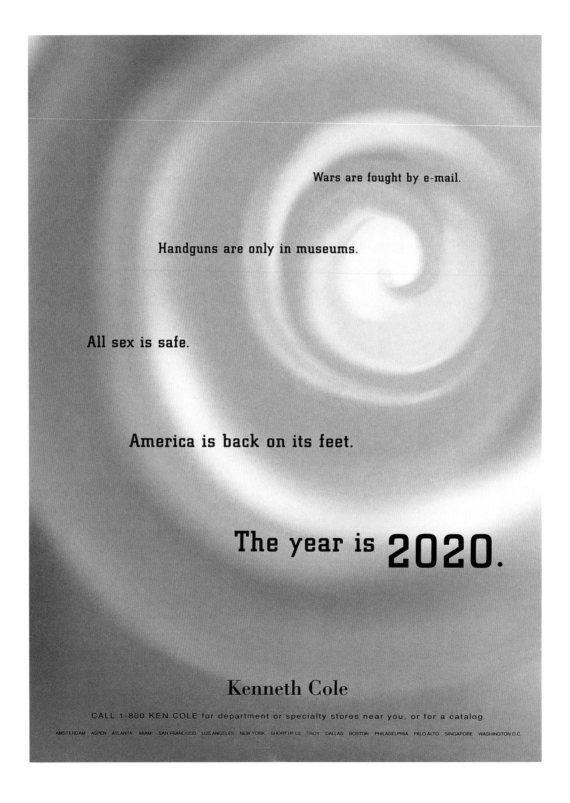

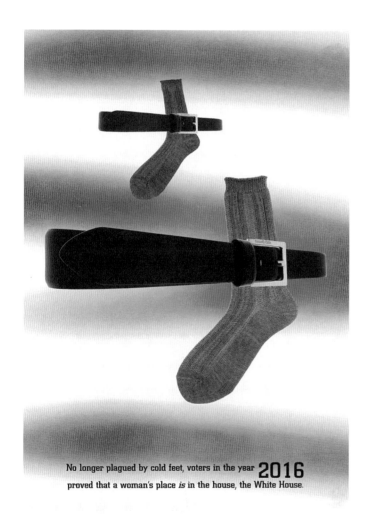

No longer plagued by cold feet, voters in the year **2016** proved that a woman's place *is* in the house, the White House.

Oversized handbags became a necessity when Bill Gates paid off the National Debt in **2010,** sparing both Social Security and Medicare.

The election of **2008** forced the tabloids out of business when the only things found in the candidates' closets made them look better, not worse.

The assassination of a world leader in the late 90's led to the long-awaited Rabin Peace Accords of **1999**, and the establishment of strong ties worldwide.

1996 marked a turning point in history as people realized that where they stand today, determines who we are tomorrow.

The future is what you make it.

Kenneth Cole

CALL 1-800 KEN COLE for department or specialty stores near you, or for a catalog.

CHANGE
LIKE NO ONE
HAD SEEN—
THE CHANGE
OF A
MILLENNIUM—
WAS
DRAWING
NEAR. SO
WE TOOK
TO THE
STREET TO
HEAR WHAT
PEOPLE
HAD TO SAY
ABOUT IT.
AFTER ALL,
A MILLENNIUM
IS WHAT
YOU MAKE IT.

1999 fall fashion
show video.

eight

THE MESSAGE IS THE MEDIUM

I have always used advertising to distinguish myself from the competition. Of course, selling anything begins with the product, and when all is said and done, it's not about the box but what's in it. The product needs to be exceptional, or at least appear to be, and it must fill a need; or maybe it *creates* a need that it then fills. Maybe the product is the first of its kind, incomparable to all others, and therefore noteworthy. The right product will be its own best salesman and its own best ad. What does it matter whether you have the best product available? If nobody knows about it, does it even exist? Does there need to be some potential demand to justify the impending supply? And what role, if any, should advertising play?

I've already mentioned that my father had a different feeling about advertising. "Bad idea," he used to tell me. "People will think you don't have confidence in your own product, or that you need business."

In some respects, I agree. More often than not, I believe traditional advertising is the worst course, and there are definitely more efficient ways of communicating a product's worth to a customer. Good public relations is significantly more effective than advertising, for a simple reason: the things that others say about you are usually more convincing than anything you can say about yourself. Point of sale marketing—meaning display, and packaging of the product, anything that happens at or near the cash register—is an ideal time to speak to the customer: the moment the crucial shopping decision is actually made. The best of all promotion is word of mouth. Every sale is potentially an unpaid endorsement, and a satisfied customer will most likely spread the word.

In fashion, there is something very appealing about *not* advertising. By not defining yourself, you remain open to interpretation. Your customers may feel as if *they* have discovered you, rather than the other way around. They can infer what they want about you, and see you the way they would like you to be.

RIGHT: A post 9/11 message.

1992 THE BERLIN WALL IS COMING DOWN. THE WORLD IS NOW DIFFERENT IN MANY WAYS.

The Berlin Wall.

"Now there's nothing to keep anyone from coming to our Semi-Annual Sale." -Kenneth Cole

Starting Thursday Dec. 7th.
Men's and Women's shoes at 30% to 50% savings.

New York
353 Columbus Ave.
(at 77th St.)

San Francisco
2078 Union St.

There's also a major downside to traditional advertising. If you do run an ad that is not better than most, you've done yourself a disservice. A bad ad is at best embarrassing and, at worst, damaging to the business; for all practical purposes, a mediocre ad is no better than a bad one: you define yourself as a mediocre company, compromising the relationship with your customer and, worse, you spend money to do it. So I have a rule: only run ads that we believe are great.[26]

A truly great advertisement satisfies three criteria: it gets the right message to the perfect place at the ideal time. A great message at the wrong time is bad; but even at the perfect time, a great message in the wrong place is no better. What works on a New York bus could be awkward on an L.A. billboard and downright insulting on a London taxi.

Advertising I believe is an opportunity to introduce your point of view, as well as to define the nature of the relationship you'd like to have with the customer. And it can even be a chance to say something important.[27] What is important? To me, current events, much of the time; laughter, often; thinking, always. I try to bring those three elements together. Humor, for me, has always been effective in allowing customers to consider its message without dogma. With humor I try to fuse, for example, global concerns with fashion realities, without trivializing either, and without being confrontational. Hopefully the ads eschew preaching, and encourage the humble opinions of writer and reader alike. I'm convinced that, deep down, most people are smart, and deeper down, they want to be treated that way. Intelligent advertising provides a vehicle for us to talk about what's already on our minds.

Since timing is everything in advertising, taking on subjects that change from day to day requires some courage, and a lot of spontaneity.[28] Whether or not an ad strikes the right tone often depends on where it is placed and when it will be seen. A mind stuck waiting for traffic to move will have a very different reaction to a message

FOOTNOTE #26
IT ALL ADS UP

At the start we didn't have an advertising budget because we didn't need one: when we thought of something worth saying, we'd take it to the press. When we had two things to say, we'd do it twice. Now that we're a public company with many business agendas, we have an in-house advertising department, an advertising schedule, and yes, an advertising budget. Which means that our process is less spontaneous, so we have to invest even more time and energy to make sure that we always have something relevant to say.

LESSON: *Plan to be spontaneous tomorrow.*

FOOTNOTE #27
9/11—THE MORNING AFTER

September 11 was a defining moment for all of us. The entire world watched, dumbfounded, as New York City was thrown into smoke-filled chaos. Most Americans slipped into a state of shock. We had discovered, in a very real and brutal way, just how vulnerable we really were.

Then, as day after day went by, and only a few people were recovered, a stillness descended over us. Out of respect for the grief that the disaster had caused, stores all over the nation had closed; in New York City, they stayed closed longer. No one wanted to shop or be seen shopping; it seemed like a trivial activity in a time fraught with real worries.

Unfortunately, the effect this had on the fashion industry in New York was devastatingly real. The market froze. Inventory backed up. Retail stores were petrified. Store windows emptied. Everyone down the line, from designers to marketers to factory workers, felt the impending threat of unemployment.

I knew if I could do anything—help in any small way—it would be to collaborate with whomever I could to encourage the public to get on with their lives. We needed to generate traffic by getting people back into stores. But how could we ask people to go shopping and still be respectful of the mourning process?

The goal of a terrorist attack is precisely to interfere with everyday, commonplace activities. Fear makes normalcy impossible, and can even make such carefree activities as shopping, exercising, or even laughing seem disrespectful.

So we chose action. Our advertising relationship with customers had always been based on real-world events. While many store windows stayed empty, we quickly had the American flag up in all of our retail outlets, accompanied by a message we had long been known for: "What You Stand For Is More Important than What You Stand In." All we had to do in this instance was to change the icon from an AIDS ribbon to the American flag. The response felt appropriate, and at the same time consistent with our roots.

American flags dotted every street in the country, and people proudly identified themselves as American. We were still uncertain if we were starting to get our national sense of humor back.

"Red, White & Blue. It's the new black," read our billboards across the country. "God Dress America," others said, asking people to come into our store and support the September 11th Fund by buying the CFDA (Council of Fashion Designers of America) T-shirts. While the tone in both ads was lighthearted, we attempted to project a tone of irony and resilience.

That November, as we were brainstorming about our spring ad campaign, one thing became quickly apparent: September 11 was still foremost in all our minds. Our creative group discussions yielded nothing more relevant, so we set out to find a new way to address the catastrophe—and very quickly realized we couldn't. Every minute of that terrible day had been examined in microscopic detail, and everyone from news anchors to psychics to televangelists offered their opinions on what it all meant.

Instead we decided to talk about something that had been ignored: the day after. On September 12, I believe we all changed in very profound ways—many of which were for the better. Our ad campaign expressed some of those sentiments:

"On September 12, people who don't speak to their parents forgot why."

"On September 12, drivers waved at fellow drivers with all 5 fingers."

"On September 12, we used protection in the bedroom, not in the mailroom . . ."

But some things never changed:

"On September 12, 14,000 people still contracted HIV."

The ad ran, and an article by a *Daily News* writer followed, accusing us of exploiting the emotions of the moment. Fox and CNN picked up on it. It wasn't an argument we felt we should pursue. In the end, other editorials defended our position, and noted that we were doing what we always did. Could we have done it better? Maybe. Was it a mistake to have done it? I don't think so.

It may still take months, or for some, forever, before New Yorkers can hear a siren and not flinch, or see a plane flying over the city and not shudder. As a businessman, I felt my own priorities shift as the city shifted around me. Prior to September 11, I always felt that we needed to control everything, to have all the variables in the business in some kind of order. Over the course of the next few days, and even months, I came to realize that no matter how much we controlled what was within our four walls, there could always be an occurrence outside those walls that defied imagination. I realized as a human being that if we couldn't respond to this crisis in a way that felt real, we could never feel good about who we were. The **LESSONS** *we learned that fateful day could fill volumes.*

KENNETHCOLE.COM

GOD DRESS AMERICA!
-KENNETH COLE

*We support Fashion for America™ T-shirts. Net proceeds will benefit the Twin Towers Fund.

POST 9/11 BILLBOARDS: Everyone was saying we needed to move forward, so we did, in the only way we knew how; openly.

KENNETHCOLE.COM

RED, WHITE & BLUE.
It's the new black. -Kenneth Cole

HAPPY 2002.

SEPTEMBER 11, 2001
at 8:47 AM. It was one of
those "man on the moon,"
"President Kennedy has been
shot" days; the kind you will
always remember where you
were and exactly what you
were doing. Among many
other things, it also happened
to be the day after our bi-
annual runway show. And it
wasn't until several months
later when we ran across
this image in a magazine,
photographed on the streets
of NYC on 9/11, that we
realized we never even
looked at the reviews that
day. An absolute crucial post-
show ritual couldn't have
been less important.

ON SEPTEMBER 12,
DRIVERS WAVED AT FELLOW DRIVERS
WITH ALL 5 FINGERS...

ON SEPTEMBER 12,
PEOPLE WHO DON'T
SPEAK TO THEIR PARENTS
FORGOT WHY...

ON SEPTEMBER 12,
WE USED PROTECTION IN THE BEDROOM,
NOT IN THE MAILROOM...

TODAY IS NOT A DRESS REHEARSAL.

EVERYONE WAS TALKING ABOUT WHERE WE WERE ON 9/11, NOT WHERE WE WERE ON 9/12.

ON SEPTEMBER 12,
14,000 PEOPLE
STILL CONTRACTED HIV...

FOOTNOTE #28
SOMETIMES SHIRT HAPPENS

When we first started doing ads in response to topical news, we put them in monthly magazines. We ran into a little problem, however: it was hard to keep the ad relevant over a magazine's three-month lead time (as well as its month on the stands). Because news travels fast and tag lines age quickly, we could go from being relevant to immaterial in a matter of days. Even with weekly magazines, it was hard to stay timely. Then we decided we'd try to react to daily news events within *hours*—the ultimate challenge—knowing that the ideal message may only stay around for the day that followed.

So we made an ad commitment on page three of the *New York Times*, a coveted advertising spot, small (three-by-five) but prominent. There, we would be speaking to a smarter, more ironic audience, who would hopefully appreciate our message.

In 1997, at the height of the Clinton-Lewinsky scandal, after many months of prying, intrusions, and relentless coverage, the President was going to take the witness stand, and there was a lot of debate about how he'd be portrayed and whether or not he should be cross-examined. We had also recently introduced men's sportswear and wanted to show New York one of our new polycotton short-sleeved shirts. Our take on it read: "Opening arguments, cross-examinations, who gives a shirt?"

We sent the ad by the usual channels on Wednesday evening and, to our surprise, received a call from an advertising executive at the *New York Times*.

"We can't run it," he told us.

"Why?" we said.

He said, "It doesn't pass our standard test of appropriateness. We don't want to offend people, and we'll need something else from you. You've got an hour to get it to us."

It was early Wednesday night, and suddenly we were scrambling. The beauty (and now, the peril) of our daily campaign was that we didn't write the ads until the day before; we had never imagined that an ad might be rejected just hours before deadline. We didn't have time to rewrite anything and, worse, we had to pay for the space whether we used it or not.

By the time my office found me, it was 7:30 P.M.

I called the advertising manager personally, and told him that there was no feasible way we could create another ad before their deadline. "And frankly," I added, "I don't think there's anything wrong with this ad. You should run it."

In an effort to not alienate a good customer, he suggested I speak directly to the advertising acceptability manager.

So I called him. By now, it was past eight o'clock. I launched into my speech, telling him he was not being reasonable, and even in a worst-case scenario, what he was dealing with was a gray area, and gray areas are defensible. I made my case in several calls. Finally, at eleven o'clock, I realized that the deadline had passed, and he was still on the phone. But at the end of the conversation, he ultimately said that he just couldn't do it. "What I can do," he offered, "is to move your ad to Friday, and put a Friday ad in your Thursday spot. And if you want to personally speak to the owner, Mr. Arthur Sulzberger, Jr., in the morning . . ."

The next morning I opened the paper to see what the replacement ad was, and there, on page three, was our original ad, in all its glory. I couldn't believe it. Apparently, by the time the editor had hung up the phone the night before, it was too late to switch the ads.

The whole exchange reinforced several beliefs. *First, always stand up for what you believe in. Second, if you run into an obstacle, keep moving—chances are you'll find a way around it. and third, don't lose faith—even when shirt happens.*

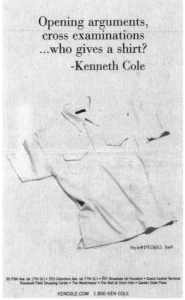

Opening arguments,
cross examinations
...who gives a shirt?
-Kenneth Cole

Style#1955015 S+9

95 Fifth Ave. (at 17th St.) • 353 Columbus Ave. (at 77th St.) • 597 Broadway (at Houston) • Grand Central Terminal
Roosevelt Field Shopping Center • The Westchester • The Mall at Short Hills • Garden State Plaza

KENCOLE.COM 1.800 KEN COLE

than a mind on vacation waiting for baggage (even though we all have baggage). As people inhabit different spaces, their ability to be engaged fluctuates, so I always think carefully about where the viewers are emotionally in their day, and how best to talk to them. An ad that is read on the way into work along New York's West Side Highway will gather a different kind of attention than an ad read by a tourist in New Orleans on the way to the French Quarter. When selecting a venue for advertising, I am sensitive to its environment: who are my neighbors and where is the neighborhood. In product positioning, as in life, you are defined by the company you keep.

The best ads are often the ones the viewer may not understand right away. They provoke thought, stir things up, and then hover in the air for an extended pause. If a message stays in a viewer's mind for only ten to fifteen seconds, that still may be twice the attention ads usually get. With the right campaign you essentially could double the return on your investment. If the message lingers longer and goes so far as to generate conversation, that value grows exponentially.

The average person is inundated with headlines daily, and suffers from information overload. So, we seek to add a somewhat rational, humorous, and occasionally credible voice to the mix, to help keep things in perspective.

Case in point: in 1992, when our competitors were using glossy, multi-page inserts to capture the attention of their audience, we went in the opposite direction. In a sort of rebellious manner we ran what we called "Anti-Ad" ads: pithy comments I scrawled by hand across fax paper (which also happened to be more affordable). The message was that we were spending no money and very little time on the ads (which was as big a message as whatever else we were saying) (See pp. 134–35.)

"We briefly considered running an 8 page ad with half-naked models, shot by a famous photographer in some exotic location."—Kenneth Cole.

"Who has time for ads? There's a sale *going on."—Kenneth Cole*

At long last we will no longer have to stare aimlessly at an empty conveyor belt wondering if our luggage was lost. Be careful what you wish for.

81%: believe the media exposes too much.
67%: still watch.
-Kenneth Cole
www.kennethcole.com 1-800 ken cole

"Buckle Up, it's the law."
-Kenneth Cole
NORTH PARK CENTER www.kencole.com
1-800 KEN COLE

3 out of 5 car accident victims wind up in suits.
-Kenneth Cole
WWW.KENCOLE.COM 1-800 KEN COLE

48%: take the parkway.
87%: prefer the belt way.
-Kenneth Cole
www.kennethcole.com 1-800 ken cole

Violent crime is down 7%.
White collar crime, up 15%.
-Kenneth Cole
WWW.KENCOLE.COM 1-800 KEN COLE

THERE'S NO TIME LIKE THE PRESENTS.
-KENNETH COLE
KENNETHCOLE.COM
HAPPY HOLIDAYS

88%: make judgements based on colour.
26%: do so in regards to clothing.
-Kenneth Cole
www.kencole.com 1-800 ken cole

"Help save the environment. Travel in pairs."
-Kenneth Cole

"Grand Opening."
-Kenneth Cole

at the galleria

67%: read billboards while driving.

31%: look out!

-Kenneth Cole

KENNETHCOLE.COM

OPEN. CLOTHES.
-KENNETH COLE

SOUTH BEACH / DADELAND / BOCA RATON / WEST PALM BEACH (opening soon)

2%: have been involved in a criminal act.

43%: have used an accessory.

-Kenneth Cole

www.kencole.com   1-800 ken cole

38%: des hommes exagèrent leur taille.

63%: sont fiers de leur stature.

-Kenneth Cole

www.kencole.com   1-800 ken cole

ACT YOUR SHOE SIZE.
SWITCH TO DECAF.
OUTFIT CHANGE. -KENNETH COLE

KENNETHCOLE.COM   1-800 KEN COLE

1992

THE RODNEY KING VERDICT [NOT GUILTY], UNCONTROLLABLE FIRES AND THE BIGGEST EARTHQUAKE TO HIT A U.S. CITY IN 50 YEARS ALL SEEMED TO SHAKE L.A. IN THE SAME WEEK.

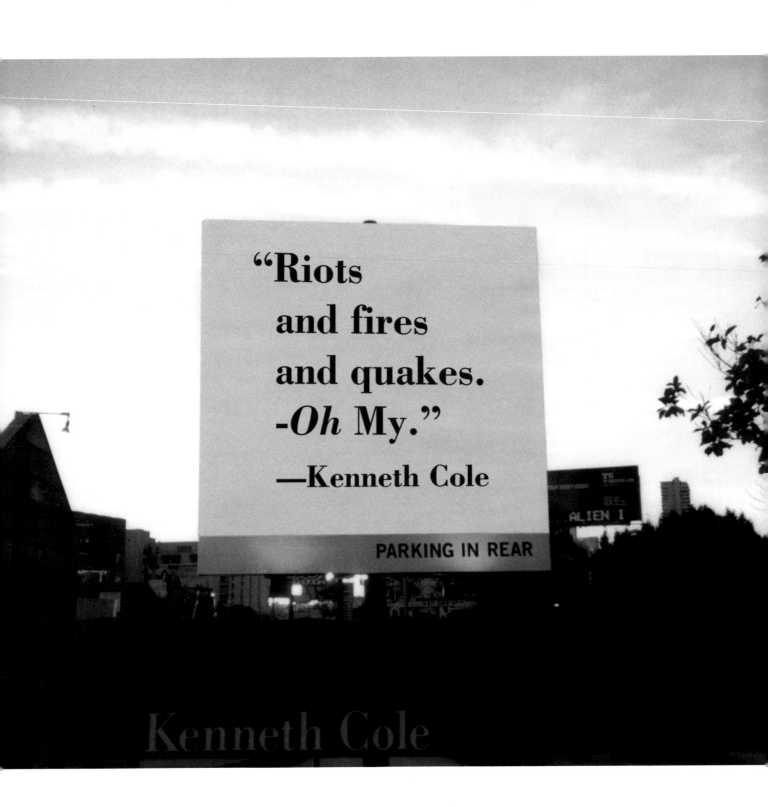

Yet another, in 1992, after the global warming summit had unleashed some scary predictions on our planet's future, in a special insert that went into ten major newspapers around the world, including the *New York Times*, we published the message:

"Is it me, or is it warm in here?"—Kenneth Cole

I have also believed that a mass, generic message can be as unappealing as the wrong message, which is why we have always taken the time to pay extra attention to who was reading what we had to say. When we opened a store in Chicago, we were careful to note how the former home of Al Capone might take to our coming:

"Just what Chicago needs, another outfit from New York."—Kenneth Cole (See p. 78.)

Numerous venue-specific ads followed, as we expanded our retail presence around the country. Each time, we sought to initiate a conversation with the various communities, in their language and on their terms.

Statistics, a universal language, have also worked well for us in advertising: they are nonconfrontational but effective. I don't expect to change people's minds just by telling them how I feel; nonetheless, a lot of change can arise out of awareness. By supplying relevant facts about key issues, as in our campaigns about gun control and the death penalty, I have offered readers the tools to change their own minds, should they be so inclined. Now, are you going to believe my statistics? That's up to you. After all, 42 percent of other people's statistics are made up (94 percent are likely to believe this, and 6 percent will invariably remain undecided). (See pp. 136–37.)

Anyway, it's my soapbox, and for better or worse, I'm standing on it.

FOOTNOTE #29
NOT OUR FAULT

It was August 1993 and our first L.A. store was about to open, well beyond our target date. We posted a billboard in front of the store that read:

"Opening by October or before San Andreas, whichever comes first."

We also ran several local ads with a photo of an earthquake, that said, "The last thing L.A. needs is another grand opening."

We eventually opened in November. Less than sixty days later, on January 17, 1994, Los Angeles was struck with the first major American earthquake in fifty years. It measured 6.7 on the Richter scale, and left behind many millions of dollars in damage. I guess the message is, *Beware of what you wish for.*

"The last thing L.A. needs is another grand opening."

——Kenneth Cole

P.S.- Now that we've opened on Sunset, let's hope San Andreas won't do the same.
8752 Sunset Boulevard, West Hollywood

AMSTERDAM   NEW YORK   SAN FRANCISCO   LOS ANGELES

SOMEWHAT

TO BE /\ CLEAR. IT WAS NOT JUST WHAT WE SAID, BUT THE WAY IN WHICH WE SAID IT.

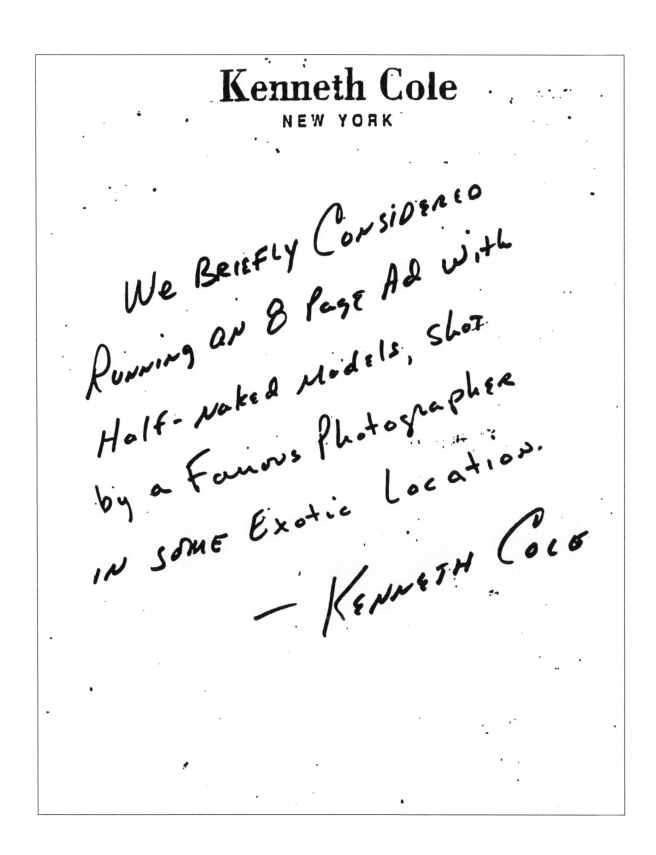

Kenneth Cole
NEW YORK

We Briefly Considered Running an 8 Page Ad with Half-naked Models, shot by a Famous Photographer in some Exotic Location.

— Kenneth Cole

100 PEOPLE CONTRACT HIV EVERY 10 MINUTES.

To be aware is more important than what you wear. —Kenneth Cole

www.kencole.com   1 800 ken cole

4 OUT OF 5 TOURISTS LOOKING FOR SOHO ARE IN IT.

To be aware is more important than what you wear. —Kenneth Cole

www.kencole.com   1 800 ken cole

1 IN 27 PEOPLE EXECUTED IS LATER PROVEN INNOCENT.

To be aware is more important than what you wear. —Kenneth Cole

www.kencole.com   1 800 ken cole

4 OUT OF 5 PEOPLE WHO WITNESS A CRIME DO NOTHING.

To be aware is more important than what you wear.—Kenneth Cole

www.kencole.com   1 800 ken cole

**THE FAMILY GUN IS
MORE LIKELY TO KILL YOU THAN A STRANGER.**

To be aware is more important than what you wear.—Kenneth Cole

www.kencole.com   1 800 ken cole

**3 OUT OF 4 NEW YORKERS
WITH TELESCOPES ARE NOT INTO ASTRONOMY.**

To be aware is more important than what you wear.—Kenneth Cole

www.kencole.com   1 800 ken cole

1999 THE INTERNET. LIKE LIFE, SOME STAYED OUT FRONT...

New York to L.A.
in 15 seconds.

www.kencole.com

KENNETH COLE PARKING IN REAR

SICK OF THE INTERNET?
GET ON-LINE.
-KENNETHCOLE.COM

OUTDOOR STEMS

WHAT ARE YOU DRIVING @?
-KENNETHCOLE.COM

SIGN REVENUES BENEFIT   INFINITY   DAVIE BOYS & GIRLS CL

AND OTHERS STAYED **BEHIND.**

AIRPLANE FOOD:
This wasn't the first time we've
been called plane nuts,
and probably won't be the last.

WE TH

SHOULD HAVE

IT COMES TO

BAREFOOT IS A

— KE

NK WOMEN

A CHOICE WHEN

EING PREGNANT.

NOTHER STORY.

NETH COLE

nine

WHAT YOU STAND FOR
EVEN
IS^MORE IMPORTANT THAN WHAT YOU STAND IN

Three years after its inception, Kenneth Cole Productions was going strong and growing stronger. But in 1985, it seemed the air was changing. The United States was beginning to experience an economic downturn and, as the Asian economies began to soar, Americans were facing the reality of longer work-weeks and still higher unemployment. As a country, we had to reorient ourselves to be more competitive, more efficient, and more resourceful. Our farmers were in crisis as they struggled to protect their family farms against foreclosure. A drought and subsequent famine in Ethiopia was killing tens of thousands, and a new, deadly disease was emerging all over the world, without a cure in sight.

But there was something else going on, too. A pervasive consciousness, a sense of activism that had not been seen since the 1960s was sweeping the United States. The idea that we could collectively impact these tragedies was mobilizing everyone. The song "We Are the World," produced by Quincy Jones, featured Bob Dylan, Michael Jackson, Stevie Wonder, Lionel Ritchie, and forty-some others, hit the airwaves in March 1985, followed three months later by the Live Aid benefit concerts in London and Washington, D.C., organized by Bob Geldof and starring Sting, David Bowie, Dylan, Carlos Santana, Mick Jagger, Phil Collins, and dozens more, all of this to benefit the starving nation of Ethiopia. Later came Hands Across America, inspiring millions of Americans to join together. It was clear that people wanted to get involved with causes that were bigger than themselves.

At the time I was contemplating ways to better connect with our customers, and wondering how to do something meaningful myself. It seemed to me that, if we as a community could care that passionately

RIGHT: Sometimes the fewest words make the biggest statement.

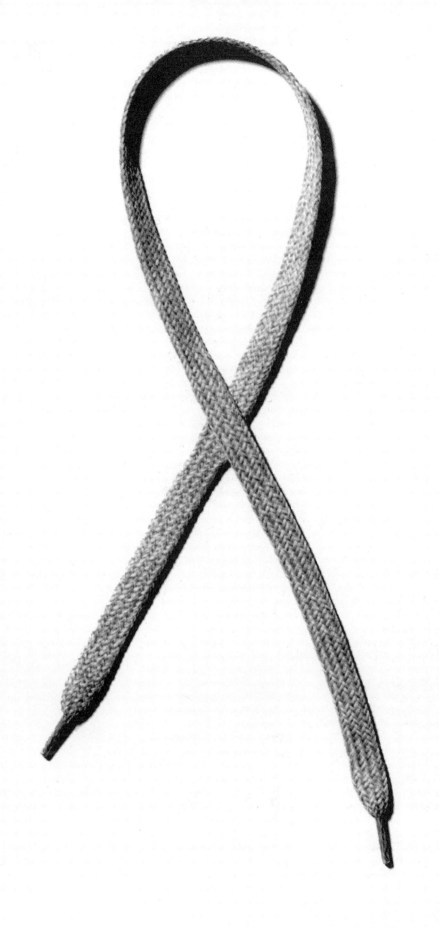

—Kenneth Cole

For the future of our children...
Support the American Foundation for AIDS Research. We do.

SEND CONTRIBUTIONS TO: AMERICAN FOUNDATION FOR AIDS RESEARCH, BOX C, NEW YORK, NEW YORK 10116

Contributors: Apollo Studios, Inc. Linda Cantello (make-up) Jenny Capitain (stylist) Elite Models Faith Kates Grace Kent Sage, Inc. Advertising
Mariella Smith-Masters (make-up) Pipino Buccheri Salon (hair stylists) PMK, Inc. (public relations) Regent Air Lines Wilhelmina Models, Inc.

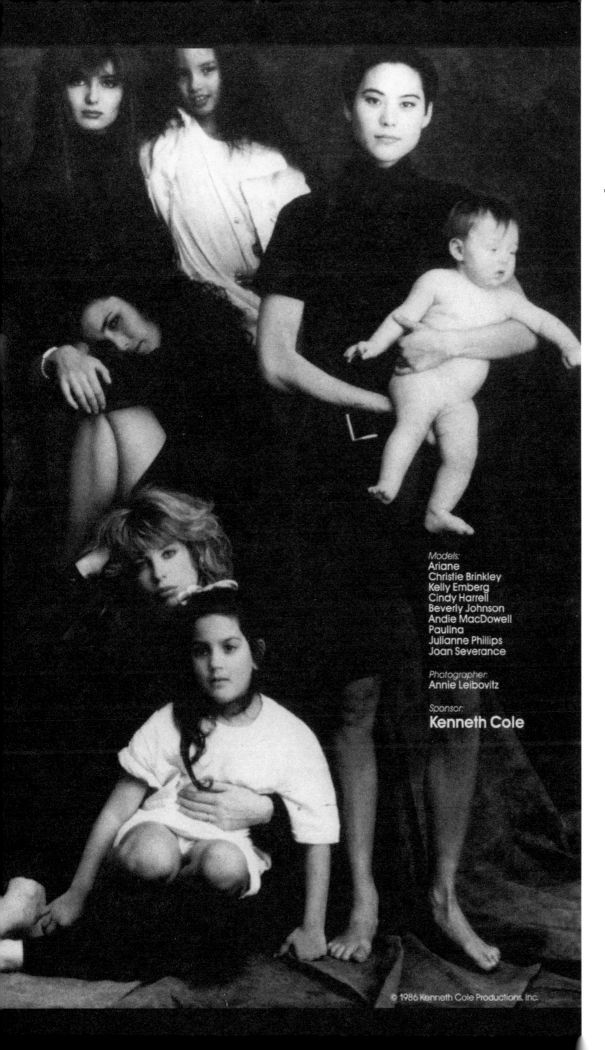

1986

OUR FIRST AD PROMOTING AIDS AWARENESS. UNFORTUNATELY, 17 YEARS LATER, NOT OUR LAST.

Models:
Ariane
Christie Brinkley
Kelly Emberg
Cindy Harrell
Beverly Johnson
Andie MacDowell
Paulina
Julianne Phillips
Joan Severance

Photographer:
Annie Leibovitz

Sponsor:
Kenneth Cole

December 1988.

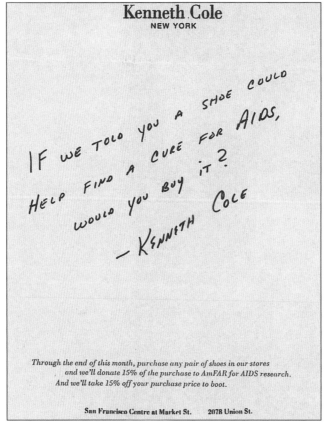

September 1992.

about the well-being of starving Ethiopians, so geographically and culturally remote from us, we could surely address something that was potentially even more devastating, and destined to touch us all soon. HIV/AIDS.

In 1985, AIDS was more than a physical disease, it was also a sociocultural disease. It robbed people of their livelihoods, their families, and their dignity. Unlike the starving of Africa, or farmers in the United States, the earliest victims of AIDS received little sympathy. A murky cloud of misinformation surrounded the disease and led to a climate of paranoia and blame. We knew it was infectious, and we knew how it was spread. In fact, much of the country felt that the victims—at the time, primarily gay men and IV drug users—brought it upon themselves through their own actions.

It may be hard to imagine now, but in those days, the fear of standing up on behalf of people with AIDS was acute. The voices that were heard were mostly within the at-risk communities, who were rallying to raise money for the humane treatment of the afflicted. Few outside these communities were advocating research, mobilizing resources to find a cure, or advancing public education to reduce the stigma affecting those already traumatized.

As a young, single, male fashion designer living in New York, I was often assumed to be one of the at-risk group. Young men in my industry were becoming infected at an alarming rate.[30] At the same time, because I was not gay and not infected with HIV, I naively believed that I had a special opportunity to say something important that could, in a small way, increase public awareness. Because, sad but true, when victims of circumstance call for change, their demands can be perceived as self-serving. The message is often broadcast more credibly by those not suffering directly.

FOOTNOTE #30
TO A FRIEND'S AIDS

David Brugnoli was an affable, easygoing, and hardworking friend who had an important role in the early years of our company. He helped design the trailer for our Shoe Show debut, and he designed our first showroom and my first retail store. Extraordinarily talented, creative, and entrepreneurial in his approach to life and circumstances, David was also gay and nonmonogamous.

As I became more conscious of and sensitive to the AIDS crisis, I began to worry about his well-being, and I asked him if he had ever gotten tested. He said no.

I asked him if he was insane.

At that point he said that there was nothing to worry about, but we both knew that wasn't true. He also said that, in his mind, there was no reason to get tested: if he was HIV-positive, it would only further complicate an already complicated existence. (Fearing he could potentially frighten and unnerve his friends and neighbors, and maybe lose his insurance, he refused to be tested.)

Then one day he showed me a huge red welt on his leg. He still wouldn't get tested and fell deeper into denial. I didn't see him very much after that day—he, like many others in his situation, didn't want to see anyone. More to the point, he didn't want anyone to see him: the stigma was too enormous. He died about six months later.

I often think that if David had just been tested early on, that if he had known how deadly his illness was, that he might have been more cautious with his personal lifestyle and still be around today.

I cared about change for two reasons. I cared because I saw what the silence was doing to my community and friends, and I cared because I wanted my small company to be part of something meaningful. No one knew then (or for that matter, now) how to cure AIDS, but we all knew how to contain it, and that was all about awareness. I felt we had an opportunity to make an impact, even though we were just a small company with an advertising budget of a few hundred thousand dollars. That amount is next to nothing in the universe of advertising, but it was a few hundred thousand more than anyone else was looking to spend to promote this crucial message at this critical time.

The truth was, all of America was suffering from the AIDS epidemic in 1985, though it would take another decade for most of us to realize it. I felt that if AIDS was half as dangerous as we had been led to believe, it stood to infiltrate every single segment of our culture.

I hoped to create a message that would bring that reality home. Infected gay men and IV drug users

Latest AIDS statistics: 40,000,000 infected.

00,000,000 cured.

were getting very little sympathy and I didn't think public perception of AIDS victims was likely to change on its own. In my mind, the community needed to rally and protect itself, and the only way that was going to happen was if certain stereotypes were thrown out the window. Everyone needed to know that they were at risk: gay men and straight men, drug users and non–drug users, men and women, adults and children.

I started by enlisting the formidable photographic talent of Annie Leibovitz who helped organize a major effort for an ad that I wanted to create. Her credibility, I hoped, would give our tentative plans for a campaign enormous critical clout. I also enlisted support of a new AIDS organization just being formed, called amfAR. An advertising friend from my El Greco/Candie's days, Grace Sage, and another friend, Faith Kates, then a model agent at Wilhelmina (and now CEO of the NEXT Agency), also jumped in, and we began making calls: Christie Brinkley (then eight months pregnant), Paulina Porizkova (on every magazine cover at the time), Andie MacDowell (top model and actress), Beverly

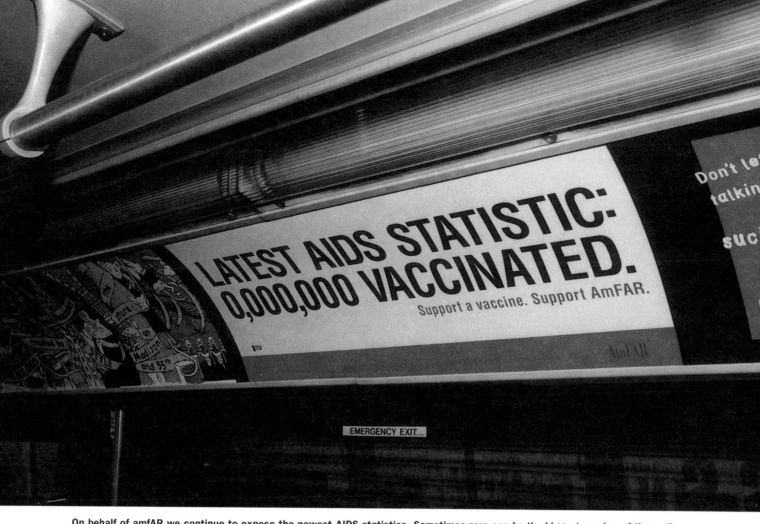

On behalf of amfAR we continue to expose the newest AIDS statistics. Sometimes zero can be the biggest number of them all.

THINK NEGATIVE.
-KENNETH COLE

SAY NO TO HIV.

Johnson, Ariana, Kelly Emberg, Joan Severance, and Cindy Harrell.

When no one committed quickly, we spoke to their bookers/agents. One thing led to another. We told Christie's agent that Paulina was more than likely going to do it, mentioned to Paulina's agent that Andie was most likely going to do it, we informed Andie's agent that Paulina was thrilled about the project, and assured Joan's agent that Christie was trying to change her plans. Kelly Emberg's agent, Molly, jumped in and also suggested another client of hers, Julianne Philips (actress, model, and at that time, recently married to Bruce Springsteen). Once we had a few important names, the rest started calling us. Soon, we had most of the current supermodels offering to donate their time to the worthy project. Hair and makeup artists, the studio, and even the car services all offered their support pro bono as well.

Then came the children. While the women's beauty and fame would draw attention to the ad, the faces of children I believed could potentially do more to destigmatize the disease than any amount of celebrity support.

To avoid any chance that the ad would be seen as exploitive, I knew we couldn't have our shoes in the photo. But if the models were not going to wear our shoes, I clearly couldn't let them wear anyone else's, so everyone went barefoot.

The ad copy ultimately read:

"For the Future of Our Children . . . Support the American Foundation for AIDS Research. We do."

On December 8, 1985, after four hours of shooting, we all finally packed up and headed home, and I readied myself for the next challenge: getting the ad seen. We decided it had to be a double page to be noticed, and I knew that, with our small budget, we wouldn't likely be able to get the ad in front of nearly enough people to have a meaningful impact. At that time, pro bono advertising was not popular among the media, but still we went to all the magazines, one at a time, to see what we could do about that. Condé Nast, after several meetings, agreed to a one-for-one deal, meaning they would match us for every ad we funded. Hearst was more generous, giving us a three- and sometimes four-for-one deal after less negotiation.

As wind of the ad got out, I started getting calls from many new, local, and underground publications that offered to run it for nothing. Every magazine contributed ad space, except for one. Ironically, it was *Interview*, founded by Andy Warhol—who had started in the art world designing shoes, and who knew many more people with AIDS than I did. A company representative explained, "If we do this for you, next we'll have to do it for the ASPCA."

The ad ended up running in twenty-three magazines (sometimes two or three times) across the country over a ten-month period from March to December 1986. We geared up for the inevitable backlash, for the fear and hatred that accompanied any association with AIDS—but it never came. We'd put our message out there in a careful and deliberate way, with the hope that certain public misperceptions of the disease would be revised.

I had started the venture as a person in tune with the times, and as a member of society who wanted to be a part of something larger than my small business. I also knew this was a strategic move for us, given the breadth of our exposure and our limited budget. Our few hundred thousand advertising dollars had in fact turned into two- to three-million-dollars' worth of exposure and much more in unpaid PR, addressing the potential impact of HIV/AIDS on *all* of our communities. What I hadn't counted on was how deeply it was going to affect me personally.

Right from the start, our AIDS ad had pushed the boundaries in advertising, talking about the disease when no one else was and, soon after, in a way that no one else would. By 1987, it was clear that both condoms and clean needles were essential in preventing the spread of AIDS in America. Unfortunately, it was illegal to advertise a condom, let alone to distribute clean needles. Nonetheless, we decided to create an ad featuring a condom. Although we airbrushed away the brand name, so that it would not necessarily be an ad for a condom, there still was some risk. Would it still be illegal? Would it even be recognizable? After all, in silhouette, it could look like anything—a UFO, say, or a graduation hat. But we decided that, unless you were born under a rock, you would know what it was. We ran it anyway, with the tag line:

"Shoes are not the only thing we encourage you to wear."—Kenneth Cole. Beneath that it read: *"Contact the American Foundation for AIDS Research."* (See p. 51.)

Later, in 1993, we created one of my favorite ads, and our simplest: a white shoelace draped across the page in the manner of an AIDS ribbon. Although it had no words, it said as much as any ad we had run to date.

Almost ten years after our first AIDS ad, the disease was still being spread at an alarming rate. People, however, had become desensitized to the issue of AIDS, partly because the drugs used to treat many HIV-positive people improved their standard of living, and so it made the problem easier to ignore. And

2001 AIDS AWARENESS IS ^STILL A PERVASIVE ISSUE.

1995 Not your average pro-bono, pro-phylactic billboard message.

yet *not one person* had been cured. HIV/AIDS wasn't going away—we just weren't reading about it as much. Forty million were living with it, twenty million had died from it, and fourteen thousand were still becoming infected every day.

Starting in the early 1990s, our company began designing provocative pro bono ad campaigns for amfAR, to communicate the organization's mission. The 1995 campaign was designed as a wake-up call. Bill Apfelbaum, a good friend who was running the outdoor media company TDI at the time, donated $2 million worth of media space to amfAR, in seventeen major markets. The anniversary of that contribution was celebrated for years afterward by TDI, and then by Viacom Outdoor. It was understood that my company would create the message and produce the campaign, knowing that amfAR would eventually have to approve it. We went back and forth in search of a message that would serve both their presumed needs, as well as our understanding of their actual needs. amfAR wanted to be informative and inoffensive, whereas I'm from the school that believes that it's hard to say something important without offending someone.

We were all aware of the rising number of AIDS victims, as well as the rising apathy of the general public. We wanted people to want to read about AIDS again, and we knew we might only have their attention for the amount of time it took them to watch a bus pass, or a billboard float by. The message eventually would say that nobody was immune, that it was not just "their" problem—we were all vulnerable.

Shown in bold, black letters on a stark white background, the ads were tabloidesque in exactly the way they needed to be. They were declarative, readable, digestible, and impossible to ignore. We addressed those least likely in most people's minds to be at risk with what we called the "If" campaign.

The first ad read:

IF YOUR DAD HAD AIDS HE'D NEED MORE THAN A NECKTIE NEXT JUNE

More followed:

IF YOUR MOM HAD AIDS SHE'D NEED MORE THAN FLOWERS ON MOTHER'S DAY

IF YOUR KIDS HAD AIDS YOU'D HAVE MORE TO WORRY ABOUT THAN CLEAN SOCKS

IF THE PRESIDENT HAD AIDS HE'D NEED MORE THAN JUST YOUR VOTE

as well as:

IF THE POPE HAD AIDS HE'D NEED MORE THAN JUST YOUR PRAYERS

And the last ad read:

IF YOU HAD AIDS YOU'D WANT SOMEONE TO BE RESEARCHING A CURE

The ads all had a reference to amfAR printed at the bottom. They were printed and presented to the amfAR staff, who agreed to run most of them. But the last one, about the Pope, they felt, was questionably appropriate and potentially "problematic."

When the day came for the unveiling of the ads to the press at the United Nations on World AIDS Day, I kept my commitment, and presented the campaign amfAR and I had agreed to run. However, to their surprise, I also presented the ad we had agreed *not* to run (and presented it as such). The press attention was formidable, and within twenty-four hours amfAR had received editorial coverage in most newspapers. Within a day or two, they also received a letter from the Archdiocese of New York demanding that the foundation "cease and desist from its plan to engage in the unauthorized public use of the Pope." amfAR was apologetic. I was not. I was not looking to shock people, per se—in an age of tabloid journalism how else do you get the public's attention? That remains a real challenge.

A few years later, in 1998, we ran a more subtle campaign.

"Latest AIDS statistic: 0,000,000 cured."

Two years later, another ad upped the ante. *"40,000,000 infected with AIDS; 00,000,000 cured."*

amfAR and much of the rest of the AIDS community are focused on the creation of a preventive vaccine, but to this day I have yet to be granted the license to produce maybe the most attention-getting campaign of all, one that we refer to as the SHOT campaign. Someday, you'll see these in print. Meanwhile, here's a sneak preview:

LAWYERS SHOULD BE SHOT WITH AN AIDS VACCINE

PAPARAZZI SHOULD BE SHOT WITH AN AIDS VACCINE

ALL PREGNANT WOMEN SHOULD BE SHOT WITH AN AIDS VACCINE

ALL CHILDREN SHOULD BE SHOT WITH AN AIDS VACCINE

(followed by a specific message advising people how they could help in the effort to create a vaccine).

Our involvement in the fight against AIDS has affected me very personally, as well as the company. In the fall of 1987, shortly after the first ad ran, I accepted an invitation to join amfAR's board, when it was still a fledgling organization with two tiny offices—East and West. AmfAR's founder, Dr. Mathilde Krim,

SOMEONE ELSE'S PROBLEM.

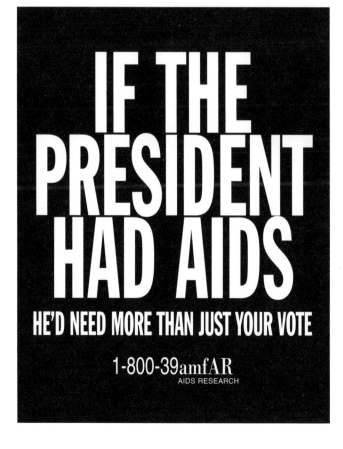

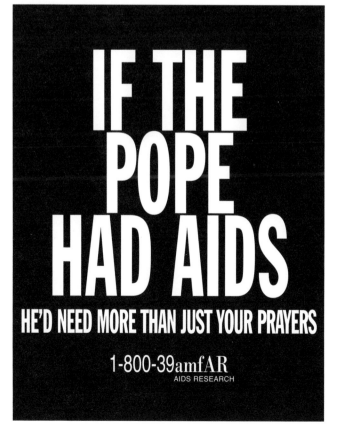

1996
In a grass roots effort to help amFAR reach a support group with minimal disposable income, we decided to speak directly to, or rather on, the disposable income. Although we defaced money, if the message came off as easily as it went on . . . was it still a crime?

a remarkable human being who continues to bring to bear all of her passion and resources, made a very flattering offer I could not refuse. Dr. Krim, Elizabeth Taylor, and many others have built amfAR into a formidable, internationally known organization that funds research, education, and advocacy for HIV/AIDS. As a director, I was asked early on to oversee amfAR's marketing and communications and, at about that time, to address an audience at Carnegie Hall.[31] Today, I hold the title at amfAR of vice chairman.

I had always considered myself somewhat of an idealist, working hard to personally realize life's rewards, but wanting to help those less fortunate than I. But in reality, in the beginning I didn't have much to offer when each exhausting day came to an end. When I started collaborating with amfAR, I had a sixty-plus-hour workweek that didn't leave time to do much more than design, sell, and market women's footwear. Then I discovered that supporting a community initiative didn't necessarily mean extending myself beyond these daily duties; it could be incorporated within them. And today, that is what sustains Kenneth Cole Productions, Inc. People come to work here because they know we are about more than selling shoes, handbags, or any article of clothing, and I imagine some customers buy our product for the same reason (and conversely, I'm sure, some do not).

We have so many obstacles to overcome in our fight against AIDS, but I remain convinced that through education, prevention, and awareness, the course of this devastating disease can be changed.

FOOTNOTE #31
A FRED BY ANY OTHER NAME

In 1986, when I began dating Maria Cuomo, I was asked to give a speech about my involvement with amfAR at Carnegie Hall, in front of four thousand members of the arts community. At first I declined; after all, I am not a public speaker—it's just not what I do or who I am. But then the organizer of the event, whom I knew as Fred, came to see me. He was so animated and persuasive that I just couldn't say no. I asked him what I was supposed to say, and he told me just to tell them what I do and why. Easy.

Maria suggested I start by thanking Fred for making the night possible; that way, she said, you won't be as nervous during the main part of your speech.

So that night, following Dr. Krim, I went up on stage at Carnegie Hall, in front of four thousand people, without notes. Because of the footlights, I couldn't see five feet in front of me, and all I could hear was the ocean of noise out there in that vast room. I started out by praising Fred, insisting that it was only thanks to Fred's effort that this event had become possible. And I seemed to be getting *great* feedback: out there in the haze, the room was buzzing. That gave me the confidence I needed to relax and just talk. I finished the speech exhilarated and relieved, grateful to Maria for her advice. When I returned to my seat, she passed me a note. "You were great. But his name is Peter."

Since then I've learned to be more careful with specifics. I recounted this anecdote at a University of Illinois convocation speech recently, and added at the end, "I hope all of you reflect back in years to come and cherish your time here at the University of Indiana."

ten

DOING WELL
BY DOING GOOD

Our early years of AIDS advocacy refocused my business priorities. I suddenly realized what an effect our commitment, personal and financial, could have on the larger community. Today I believe that getting involved is not just important for businesses: the failure to do so borders on being irresponsible. So, without wavering in my commitment to the AIDS cause, I have seized opportunities to address other social problems through our various resources including advertising, certainly the most visual and also the most effective medium I have found.

Our ads aim to make the curious *think*—to start a dialogue and shake things up a little, even if it means going where no company has gone before. But, I've learned, just because people are thinking, that doesn't mean they're always thinking what you hoped. We get letters and e-mails from all over the world, in all forms, from well-composed articulations to singular expletives, from odes of praise to loads of . . . *not* praise. But doing what we do requires a certain amount of risk taking, to push things one step further. We've taken many steps, and a few missteps, as we've worked the message into our medium.

What started organically as a personal effort and a contribution to the community as well as a business strategy has become our trademark.

Our cause-related marketing is a process that starts with meetings at the beginning of every season, where we take inventory of what concerns us today and what we believe will still be important in a few months. I go to meetings and talk about issues that have worked their way into my consciousness, in

RIGHT: Ad for annual drive, February 1998.

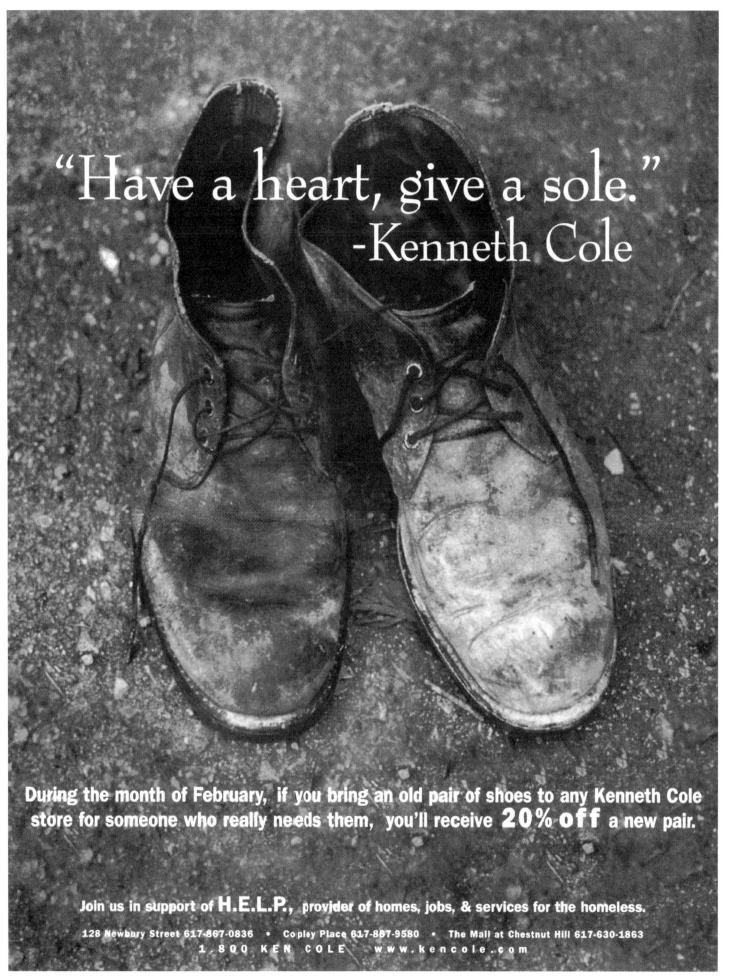

"Have a heart, give a sole."
-Kenneth Cole

no particular order of importance. I talk about what is puzzling to me, and what is pleasing, and where I think we might be headed as a community. In the absence of therapy, I rant, I rave, I eventually exhaust myself, and then I listen to everyone else do the same thing. A quiet settles over the room as we ask ourselves how we can appropriately address what is on our minds. How can we say something that hasn't been said before? What is relevant? What is meaningful today, and, even more important, in several months, when the message is likely to be seen? The discussion evolves over time.

In 1988 America had another growing epidemic. Homelessness became an enormous problem that only *increased* during the greatest period of affluence and economic growth in our country's history. While the Clinton years saw the creation of more millionaires and billionaires than any other era, they also saw the creation of more homeless Americans. By the year 2000, the richest 20 percent of the population was making 43 percent more than they made ten years before, but the poorest 20 percent were making 21 percent less in real dollars. What did that mean? What no one wanted to hear: that with all of our progress, as the rich got richer, the poor were becoming poorer and losing their homes, and their dignity, in the process.

No one wanted to hear that, and few had to—because most of America's destitute are not registered and do not vote. Over half are children, many the children of single mothers. As a board member of HELP USA, I continue to be sensitive to this growing crisis.[32] As a growing but silent itinerant community, the homeless were without a voice. We studied these realities, while looking for ways to address them:

FOOTNOTE #32

HELPING HANDS

Originally founded by my brother-in-law, Andrew Cuomo, HELP USA (formerly called H.E.L.P.—Housing Enterprise for the Less Privileged) has been directed for the past decade by my wife, Maria Cuomo Cole. I was an original board member and still sit on the board today. It was started with the belief that homelessness wasn't just a housing issue, and that the inhumane warehousing of homeless individuals and families in welfare hotels and emergency shelters wasn't bringing us any closer to solving the problem. Through the combination of shelter and supportive services, communities could address the underlying causes of homelessness. Once those causes are understood, the right means can be offered to help homeless people work toward self-sufficiency.

HELP USA is the nation's largest builder, developer, and operator of transitional and permanent housing for the homeless and low-income-earning individuals, with comprehensive on-site human services, which provide for more than 6,600 homeless people at twenty-one residences throughout the country each day.

Maria took HELP USA and added a vocational aspect to it—they implemented a culinary program, a technology program, a security program, and trained people for real jobs. In seventeen years, thousands have left HELP USA with a home, a job, and a future.

LESSON: *Give a man a fish and he eats for a day, teach him to fish and he may never again need HELP.*

Where better to raise awareness for the rising homeless problem than in the very place some actually try to raise money.

ELIZABETH TAYLOR

MEL GIBSON

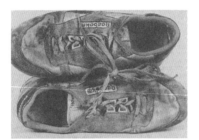

DOROTHY HAMILL

MADONNA

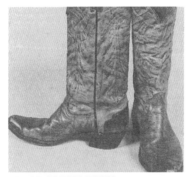

BRUCE SPRINGSTEEN

WHOOPI GOLDBERG

I HAVE TRIED TO FIND AN APPROPRIATE WAY IN THIS BOOK TO ACKNOWLEDGE THE IMPORTANT CONTRIBUTIONS OF CERTAIN INDIVIDUALS, MANY OF WHOM ARE FRIENDS WHO, OVER THE YEARS, HAVE ACQUIRED CELEBRITY STATUS AND HAVE SOUGHT WAYS TO USE IT TO BETTER OUR COMMUNITIES AND THE LIVES OF OTHERS.

BELOW ARE SOME OF THE EVENTS THAT OWE THEIR SUCCESS TO THESE INDIVIDUALS.

SOLE WORTHY

It was now 1986, and I had come to realize that we needed a larger retail presence and it had to be somewhere that would serve our growing collection and enable us to house future productions. Our stores on Columbus Avenue in New York and Union Street in San Francisco were continuing to serve their objectives, but we needed to step up and into the center of the retail world. Next stop . . . 57th Street, right off Fifth Avenue (since closed). The opening party needed to be press-worthy and as spectacular as the location. I needed to capture the attention of not just the consumer, but also the industry. It would have to be important enough, without being blatantly extravagant. It needed to also be another vehicle to remind others, but more importantly ourselves, about the raging AIDS epidemic. The resulting plan was to ask celebrities not for their time or money, but for their old shoes (it hadn't been done before to our knowledge). We would then, in the interest of AIDS research, auction them off in the perfect venue: our new store. Although it may not have attracted the most press, it was probably the most successful initiative we had undertaken to date. Within a few weeks of calling every celebrity we knew—and didn't know—I had in my possession autographed old dress sandals from Elizabeth Taylor, graffitied sneakers from Andy Warhol, shoes from Bill Cosby, Rod Stewart, Mel Gibson, and Madonna. I also had received a pair of Gregory Hines tap shoes, signed ice skates from Dorothy Hamill, cowboy boots worn by Bruce Springsteen from his "Born in the U.S.A." tour, and a horseshoe worn by Secretariat, and more.

The auctioneer was David Brenner and special appearances were made by Keith Hernandez and Ron Darling to personally auction the shoes they had just worn that week in their World Series triumph for the New York Mets.

The evening was unique and memorable. Many more New Yorkers became aware of our new store on 57th Street, and of amfAR's mission. And amfAR had about $50,000 more to invest in AIDS research.

N.Y. Met Ron Darling, Kenneth Cole, Joan Severance, David Brenner, Beverly Johnson, N.Y. Met Keith Hernandez.

CAN YOU SPARE A SOLE?

Coinciding with our annual shoe and clothing drive each February, it also happened to be the time of year that we were to take the stage before the world's fashion press. Fashion Week.

The contrast of purpose was obviously unsettling, so somewhat characteristically we interconnected the two. A fashion message that coincided with a human message.

All guests were sent invitations printed on the side of empty felt shoe bags, and those wishing to attend were asked to fill the bag and bring it with them.

On this occasion, waiting in a HELP USA van, were friends and volunteers accepting whatever was offered. Here were Maria Cuomo Cole, Billy Baldwin, and David Brenner.

On another occasion, assisting in this effort were friends Joey Pantoliano, Kyra Sedgwick, Kevin Bacon, New York Giant Michael Strahan, and New York Mets catcher Mike Piazza.

Billy Baldwin, Kenneth Cole, Maria Cuomo Cole, and David Brenner.

Joey Pantoliano, Kevin Bacon, Kenneth Cole,
Mike Piazza, and Michael Strahan.

Mohammad Ali, Michael J. Fox, Tracy Pollan,
Arnold Schwarzenegger.

THE RIGHT PARTY,
AT THE RIGHT TIME

It's the year 2000, and retail has become an even more important part of our future, and the gentrification of downtown Philadelphia became too compelling and impressive not to be part of it.

So a larger ten-thousand-square-foot store on Walnut Street became the project. The store was finally set to open by the summer of 2000 and, at the same time, our friends at the Creative Coalition were looking for a venue to host their upcoming and always impressive political convention celebrity press party. What better and more public way would there have been to show a nonpartisan but politically sensitive posture?

The party became the event of the convention with many of the elected officials attending along with Michael J. Fox, his wife, Tracy Pollan, Muhammad Ali, and Arnold Schwarzenegger. Walnut Street needed to be closed, and many, including the Bush twins, were closed out, with the help of Philadelphia's Finest.

AIDS GOES ON

AIDS outreach, AIDS awareness, AIDS fund-raising, and AIDS advocacy have become a vital part of Kenneth Cole; the man, the brand, and the business. We had launched our first AIDS awareness campaign about fifteen years earlier, and I was proud to be honored by amfAR alongside advocates Natasha Richardson and Rosie O'Donnell, and was presented the award by longtime ally and advocate Sharon Stone.

Above: At amfAR Awards with Rosie O'Donnell; Natasha Richardson; Dr. Mathilde Krim; amfAR president, Jerry Radwin; Kenneth Cole; Sharon Stone; and Nicola Bulgari. Left: A few years later, with Richard Gere and Dr. Mathilde Krim, we unveiled our most recent public service announcement; Right: At a reception for CPFA with Sharon Stone and Beverly Johnson.

FELLOW CAN YOU SPARE SOME CHANGE?

Kenneth and Robert Redford at Emory at the Kenneth Cole Fellowship conference.

In an effort to give our message of community building and social change a somewhat independent and fertile life of its own, I partnered with Emory University in January 2001. We launched the Kenneth Cole Fellowship for Community Building and Social Change, along with an Annual Leadership Conference with a similar agenda. It was our hope and intention of empowering and unleashing an elite group of individually inspired and gifted "change agents" into the world each year.

These fellows, at a relatively early age, will hopefully be empowered with the skills to identify opportunities to effect meaningful social change and find constructive and effective vehicles to make our communities better.

The inaugural conference began with a keynote address from Governor Mario Cuomo and ended with a closing address by President Jimmy Carter.

The second year's featured speaker was Robert Redford, who inspired many and influenced the introduction of an environmental component to its agenda. This conference will address a new social issue each year and will hopefully act as a national model for other universities to follow.

Mario Cuomo, President Jimmy Carter, and Kenneth Cole

THE GEORGE AWARDS

Paul Newman and John Kennedy, Jr., who have given so generously to their community, acknowledged the importance of community outreach and social change. Unfortunately, we lost John only a few months later.

Paul Newman, Kenneth Cole, and John F. Kennedy, Jr.

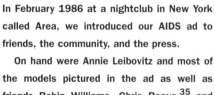

Maria Cuomo Cole, Nelson Mandela, and Kenneth Cole.

ON A JET PLANE

Returning home from New Orleans, having been there to witness the shooting of our first out-of-town ad campaign, I was generously offered a relatively larger private airplane to demo for the journey. Coincidentally, I had received a call from Dr. Mathilde Krim of amfAR the same day, wondering if by any chance I knew of a way to assist Former South African President Nelson Mandela on his travel home from Baton Rouge to New York. He was looking to return the same day at virtually the exact same time, so that we would be able to pick him up on our journey home without having to change our plans or inconvenience him in the slightest. To add even further to fate, the size of his party just so happened to be the exact number of available seats on the plane.

As he entered the plane and took his seat, I leaned over to address this extraordinary man with a question. Something like, "How were you able to maintain your drive, determination, and will, let alone your sanity, for twenty-seven years while incarcerated?"

I then sat back for the next two and a half hours, and just listened to one of the most inspiring and uplifting stories I have ever heard. His words transformed me. Remembering that trip and his story continues to inspire me. Why should any of us ever give up hope? Is anything truly insurmountable?

THE UNVEILING:

In February 1986 at a nightclub in New York called Area, we introduced our AIDS ad to friends, the community, and the press.

On hand were Annie Leibovitz and most of the models pictured in the ad as well as friends Robin Williams, Chris Reeve,[35] and Whitney Houston, who upon saying hello advised me that one of the four-inch heels she was wearing (not one of ours) had just broken in half. The unveiling had to wait until I was able to get her a new pair (one of ours).

Above: Advocates Christopher Reeve, Robin Williams, Paulina Porizkova, and Annie Leibovitz. Bottom: Dr. Mathilde Krim, Julianne Phillips Springsteen, Paulina Porizkova, and Beverly Johnson.

Despite our current economy, more homeless than fortunes are being made every day. ☹
-Kenneth Cole

FOOTNOTE #33
HEY, THAT'S ME!

A few months after our original ad ran, we were surprised to receive a letter from the homeless man featured in the ad. He was upset we had not obtained his permission before publication. We apologized for our misstep in this regard, explaining that we hadn't known where to look for him to ask for his permission, and that we had not meant to offend him. We also told him that we were starting a drive to donate clothing to men like himself. He considered the circumstances, asked for some new shoes, and we happily agreed.

The **LESSON** here is don't judge a man or his initiative by his address.

FOOTNOTE #34
THE POWER OF ONE-TO-ONE

Under the auspices of the state government, my mother-in-law, Matilda Cuomo, started a program called the New York State Mentoring Program. It was founded on the belief that if every child had a role model, the community would have an active role in improving the lives of the next generation. Matilda's program offers something for everybody: it gives kids someone to look up to, a responsible role model, and it provides busy, working people, often without kids of their own, a chance to have a meaningful relationship and give and share their values and experiences with someone who can benefit from them.

The program, now known as Mentoring USA, has become a great success. Companies like Bloomingdale's, Nickelodeon, Morgan Stanley, and, of course, KCP work to mobilize mentors. The individuals in those organizations who participate in the program are enriched by it themselves. For example, about thirty KCP employees, mostly young and single, initiated a relationship with a group of second-graders from PS 111—which I believe both mentor and mentee looked forward to every week.

LESSON: *Most of society's problems can be solved one person at a time.*

During the month of February, we'll give you 20% off a new pair of shoes when you bring in an old pair for someone who really needs them.

Kenneth Cole
NEW YORK
353 Columbus Ave. at 77th St.   95 Fifth Ave. at 17th St.

All proceeds benefit H.E.L.P. Homeless Housing Program.

FOOTNOTE #35
SUPERMAN

I have known Christopher Reeve for a long time, and was distraught, as was the entire nation, when I learned of his accident. When I saw him a few months later, he was completely paralyzed, in a wheelchair, and on a respirator.

"How are you doing?" I asked him, not knowing what else to say.

"I'm fine," he said. "But my body's not."

It amazed me that he could separate the two, even in those early months. He understood what he had lost, but he also understood what he still had, and that astonished me.

His clarity about his condition was truly inspirational, especially as he gathered his resources and power, lobbying to double the National Institutes of Health budget, testifying before the Senate in favor of federally funded stem cell research, and founding CRPF, the Christopher Reeve Paralysis Foundation. Chris's determination and strength of character have given me a lot of courage, and his actions have made him a great role model for me and many others.

LESSON: *Without the adequate use of one's body, it's extraordinary what one can still do with the right amount of one's heart.*

FACT: Most of the women and men who are homeless need jobs. To attain and maintain those jobs, they have to be dressed for a work environment.

FACT: Our customers, who have a considerable amount of disposable income, will probably have purchased at least five pairs of shoes that they do not wear or want.

FACT: If we can figure out how to give our customers an incentive to make room in their closet and at the same time help someone who can use what's in that closet, we will have helped both ourselves and our community.

So our campaign started with a picture of a homeless man and a message too blunt to be missed.[33]

"There are too many people who would love to be in your shoes."

In February 1992 the shoe drive was off and running. "Bring in a pair of shoes you aren't wearing and we'll give you a discount on a new pair," we told our customers.

And later:

- *"Have a heart, give a sole."*
- *"It's OK to shoe the homeless."*
- *"This is no time for cold feet."*

The response was overwhelming. The shoe drive, which started as a week-long event in our New York stores, has expanded over the years to become a nationwide clothing and shoe drive for the entire month of February. Today, the drive has brought in close to a million pairs of shoes, and many tons of clothing. A lot of people think clothing has nothing to do with homelessness, but nothing could be further from the truth. How good one looks often determines how one is looked at, and can provide a step toward regaining one's self-respect. It is also an integral part of professional appearance, and appearance creates perception. Someone seeking employment and a fresh start needs to look the part. I

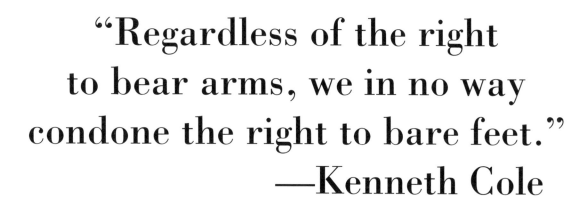

"Regardless of the right
to bear arms, we in no way
condone the right to bare feet."
—Kenneth Cole

THERE ARE MORE CHILD SAFETY REGULATIONS ON TOY GUNS THAN THERE ARE ON THE REAL THING. the family gun stands a grea_____ _f killing you than a stra_____ ARMS WAS _____ 2 ti__s WORE WHIT_____ 25 ou__r deaths a_____mbed highe_____ERICAN HOUSEHOLDS, in_____ F_____ TOY. THIS IS_____

2001
We were discouraged from mailing this invitation to our Fall 2001 runway show. Apparently, toy guns are better regulated than real ones.

hope our drive makes getting up and going out easier for many. And for our customers, the drive provides them with a reason to clean out their closet and give something valuable back to the community.

For the business, the drive stimulates our sales at just the right time. February is always a difficult time of year for clothing sales—it's still cold in much of the country, and people aren't ready to buy spring clothes yet. As a wholesaler for the better department and specialty stores, we can't sell merchandise in our own stores for a lower price than they do in theirs; it would be like biting the hand that feeds us. But what we *can* do is to provide a unique incentive for our retail customers to shop when they ordinarily might not, while adding goodwill to the brand at the same time. This enhances our brand's value, which in turn benefits our department and specialty store customers. Everybody wins.

Can it be good business to point out social failings? Conventional wisdom says no. There's a tendency to disassociate something as grave as homelessness from something as potentially glamorous as fashion. But that has never made sense to me as a businessman, nor as a human being. Consumers spend many dollars to make themselves look and feel better. Why not afford them the opportunity to spend it in a way that serves others as well?

"If we don't stand by our children,
who will follow in our footsteps?"
—Kenneth Cole

"What a feet."
—Kenneth Cole

Some say that taking care of the community is the government's job, and in many ways it is. But we all know that the government doesn't always have the will or capability to offer help to those who need and deserve it.[34] That's where the private sector comes in. I've always known, intellectually, that the private sector needs to serve the communities that support it. I've felt it personally, as well as emotionally. Still, that one step from understanding to action can be an arduous journey.

It still escapes me exactly why we took the next step, and joined the debate about gun control. Talk about stepping into an explosive issue! I guess I knew emotionally, but not intellectually, what the outcome would be. Our gun control ads have caused controversy from the start, which is something I find particularly fascinating, considering they weren't initially that controversial.

It only seems logical: just as we try to keep drunks away from cars, we need to keep the wrong people away from guns. People with compromised judgment often use both. They might perceive in the instant that they are acting appropriately, and live to regret their decisions, but unfortunately the consequences of their actions are not always theirs alone to deal with.

Our first gun control ad was released in 1986. It read:

"Regardless of the right to bear arms, we in no way condone the right to bare feet." (See p. 173.)

The ad went through twenty incarnations before we finalized it, because I did not want to be confrontational. I wanted to address the issue with my footwear credentials. We deliberated at length about how to make a point without taking a side. Regardless of how I felt, it was the art of careful wording, or, in Yogi Berra parlance: "I didn't really say what I just said." We did not condone firearms, nor did we expressly condemn them, but when it came to footwear, our position was clear.

In my mind, our original ad was explicable, defendable, defensible, and responsible. Not that I got much of a chance to explain, defend, or respond. The letters were instantaneous.

Our next several efforts were full of statistics about guns, allowing readers to draw their own conclusions. The facts speak for themselves. The victims of gun violence are often families and children:

- 16,000 kids die every year from gun violence.

- The family gun is more likely to kill you than a stranger.

- A bottle of aspirin comes with more safety regulations than a handgun.

- There are more federal regulations on a teddy bear than a handgun.

The more critical we were of unregulated handguns, although still not specifically stating our opinion or suggesting a call to action, the larger and louder the threats. However, the next campaign created the biggest stir yet. It was an ad that took the form of an open letter to gun manufacturers, and was cc'd to Charlton Heston, twenty-six governors, Kmart shoppers, the entire state of Texas, as well as gun advocacy groups. It read:

"Congratulations. We hear your product is really making a killing."

We may have gone too far here. The public debate had been more about gun safety than the existence of guns. The response was (and continues to be) a mix of praise and outrage from gun control advocates and gun enthusiasts. The latter are especially noisy. They tell me to mind my own business, to stick to fashion, to "go back to your shoes," to respect the Second Amendment, which protects their right to bear arms. And always, "Guns don't kill people, people kill people." To which I usually respond with a letter of genuine appreciation stating something to the effect "that the Second Amendment may protect their right to bear arms, but the First Amendment allows me to tell them how I feel about it." Then I go on to praise this great country we live in.

As if the gun controversy were not enough, we really stirred the pot, and I knew I must have lost my mind, when we started to talk about reproductive rights in 1992, at the height of the *Roe v. Wade* debate. This issue is an interesting one for me, because personally, I don't know if I would choose to have an abortion. Although I respect and understand the position of those for and against it, in the end I stand behind every woman's right to make that decision for herself. I don't believe a society as complicated as ours can maintain absolutes on an issue like this.

Again, despite how I felt personally, we didn't want to burden anybody with that, but we did want to clearly express our feelings about a woman's responsibility toward footwear.

The first ad we published, in 1992, read:

"We Think Women Should Have the Choice When It Comes to Being Pregnant. Barefoot Is Another Story."

Just like the gun ads, everyone read what they wanted to read, and many people assumed it said something that it didn't. We received hundreds of letters from furious pro-lifers, along with pictures of fetuses and threats. NARAL (National Abortion Rights Action League), on the other hand, offered to honor me. But, as we were quick to point out, the message in the ad is actually about family planning, with no ref-

It is a woman's right to choose.
After all, she's the one carrying it.
-Kenneth Cole

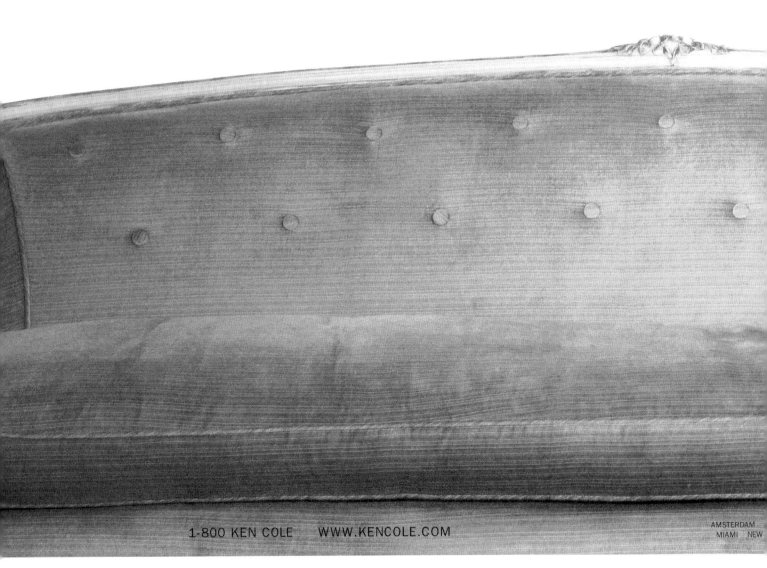

1997

WHO KNEW A LITTLE AD ABOUT WOMEN AND THEIR LOVE FOR HANDBAGS WOULD CAUSE SUCH A COMMOTION?

NTA   BOCA RATON   BOSTON   CHESTNUT HILL   DALLAS   HONG KONG   HONOLULU   HOUSTON   KING OF PRUSSIA   LAS VEGAS   LOS ANGELES
ROOK   PALO ALTO   PARAMUS   SAN DIEGO   SAN FRANCISCO   SANTA MONICA   SHORT HILLS   SINGAPORE   TAIPEI   TROY   WASHINGTON D.C.

erence to terminating pregnancy. I politely refused NARAL's offer, but I kept thinking about the debate.

Years later, another ad showed how we'd evolved: I guess it was more controversial, featuring two handbags, side by side on a couch, with the tag line,

"It is a woman's right to choose. After all, she's the one carrying it." (See pp. 178–79)

Result: more mail, more pictures, more pro-life groups rallying against us. Although I don't believe that most of the complaints came from customers, the writers often pretended to be customers to strengthen their threat. One scathing letter ranted for several paragraphs before concluding, "And I have bought my last pair of Cole Haan shoes!" I can come to terms with that. Or, "I will tell my grandchildren to never wear your products again." Not that bad, either.

That's not to say I don't take the threat of losing customers seriously. As the CEO of a public company, I don't make business decisions without a great deal of reflection. The business agenda is always considered at length, whatever my moral views. I have too many people to answer to: our customers, to convince them that our products will benefit their way of life; our shareholders, to give them something worth investing in; our employees, to provide them with steady work in a stable environment. And most importantly, I have to answer to my family and myself, and feel good about getting up in the morning and going to work.

In my earlier years I worked tirelessly to say what I thought should be said without alienating anyone in the process. I have come now to accept that you can't have it both ways. In spite of making every effort to straddle the fence, we were nonetheless bearing the brunt of what we carefully and methodically tried to *not* say. Not everyone likes what we have to say, of course. I understand that when we cross a line that is particularly sensitive, we are going to hear about it. I'd be naive to imagine that I can convince anybody how to think on a specific issue; by definition, an issue has supporters on both sides. Every letter deserves respect and attention—and a response. I respect the fact that my detractors take the time to tell me how they feel. Although, for everyone who takes the time to write a letter, I believe that there could be a hundred with the opposite opinion who don't bother to sit down and do the same. I am sure that people have been alienated by some of our messages, but I believe that many have also been inspired. And I believe that there are many more who appreciate our courage and willingness to elevate the dialogue, whether they agree or not.

By acting and reacting to real issues, and keeping an open dialogue along the way, I have pushed my business further than many others would have. And while the worst days might have me questioning what in the world I have taken on, the best days provide all the answers.

I have no regrets, no reservations, and no illegal guns.

IN THE 10 MINUTES IT TAKES THE AVERAGE PERSON

40% OF AMERICANS BELIEVE CLONING A SHEEP IS

ALMOST AS MANY SUITS ARE TRIED IN THE

THE AVERAGE AMERICAN IS ONLY 3 PAY

1 IN 5 MEN LIE ABOUT THEIR SHOE

67% OF KIDS TODAY HAVE ACCESS TO TH

WITHOUT MENTORS, KIDS ARE 80% MORE LIKE

O DRESS, OVER 100 PEOPLE WILL CONTRACT HIV.

UNETHICAL. ALTHOUGH 65% CHEAT ON THEIR MATE.

COURTROOM TODAY AS THE DRESSING ROOM.

CHECKS AWAY FROM LOSING THEIR SHIRT.

SIZE, FOR ONE REASON OR ANOTHER.

HOTTEST NEW ACCESSORY, THE FAMILY GUN.

LY TO BECOME SOMETHING IN LIFE...LOAFERS.

eleven ½

(BECAUSE NO STORY ABOUT A BUSINESS SHOULD END IN CHAPTER 11)

ON THE EDGE,
DON'T PUSH

I have learned over the years that I'm not going to get anywhere unless I extend myself; that even a slow-moving turtle knows he has to stick his neck out; that you take chances and calculated risks; that you can't make a good deal unless you are prepared to lose it; and that, yes, you leave the nest, test the water, and explore the edge. And occasionally you are going to have to jump.

Communicating my message, while trying to keep it fresh, is all about keeping an edge. The edge is the culmination of various experiences; it changes every day, shifting between known options and unknown possibilities. In the fashion business, maintaining an edge is also a strategy encompassing personal, cultural, and emotional expression, all at once. For us, the edge is also about what is cool, it is very much about urbanity. We look to the city for inspiration, the young, working chic who are constantly reinventing themselves, the action and the reaction in every moment. New York, in particular, is a place known for building and rebuilding, defining and redefining. The city, with its forceful collective heartbeat, is a creative incubator in which cool is reincarnated every day. In this business, knowing what's cool is an important consideration. A look you have seen on someone else, depending on who that someone is, could be the height of cool or it could be history.

LEFT: Scaling a New York City building just to make a point, Fall 1999.

"Shoes shouldn't have to stay in the closet either."
- Kenneth Cole

REGARDLESS OF YOUR ORIENTATION YOU SHOULD CLEAN $\underset{\wedge}{OUT}$ YOUR CLOSET.

"Come out, come out,
wherever you are."

—Kenneth Cole

And while you're out, stop by one of our stores.

While trying to serve the ongoing needs of the business, we make necessary accommodations for our target customer. Until the launch of our perfume, for example, we never did television advertising. The audience for TV reaches far beyond our target audience, and since one pays by the size of the audience, it would be inefficient, and more importantly, too "mass," and therefore possibly image-diluting. We are selective about what we create and when, what we sell and where, and what we market and to whom. We do not try to be all things to all people. After all, where a customer buys a raincoat is not necessarily the same place they want to buy their underwear (unless of course, they want them to match).

As a public company, our business needs to grow. The problem is that big business isn't cool, and small businesses don't work. So I've worked over the years to build a large business by compiling small ones, each appealing to various interests.

Equally, by sensitively addressing the different communitites we serve, our customer base has naturally come to reflect an interesting mosaic. For example, our relationship with the gay community began with our AIDS advocacy, mainly because we realized we had a common objective—to encourage responsible behavior that would slow down the spread of HIV/AIDS. It also happens that gay men tend to be more attentive to what they wear than straight men, and usually ahead of the fashion curve. We have run several ads that clearly do not speak to everyone, including:

"Shoes shouldn't have to stay in the closet either."

and

"Come out, come out, wherever you are."

As a result of this dialogue with the community, our public AIDS efforts, and overall advocacy for gay rights, I have proudly accepted awards from organizations including GLAAD, and the Human Rights Campaign.

Another niche business that we have built over the years is bridal footwear. A wedding day, I realized, is a rare opportunity to reinforce a meaningful bond with our customer. After all, women never forget who was waiting for them at the end of the aisle, as well as what they looked liked en route. What an endorsement, to be part of a never-to-be-forgotten journey!

BRIDES THE PERFECT DAY DESERVES THE PERFECT PAIR. ALSO AVAILABLE IN OFF-WHITE.

"We've been standing up brides for years."

-Kenneth Cole

Flower Girl $120

95 Fifth Ave. (at 17th St.) • 353 Columbus Ave. (at 77th St.) • 597 Broadway (at Houston)
The Mall at Short Hills • The Westchester • Roosevelt Field Shopping Center • Garden State Plaza

1.800 KEN COLE kencole.com

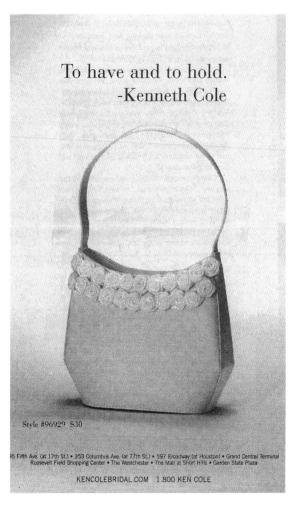

To have and to hold.
-Kenneth Cole

Style #96929 $30

95 Fifth Ave. (at 17th St.) • 353 Columbus Ave. (at 77th St.) • 597 Broadway (at Houston) • Grand Central Terminal
Roosevelt Field Shopping Center • The Westchester • The Mall at Short Hills • Garden State Plaza

KENCOLEBRIDAL.COM 1.800 KEN COLE

"There's never an excuse for cold feet."

—Kenneth Cole

I love the fashion business. I love that it often rewards my quest to do what feels right and that it overall rewards my insatiable desire to keep doing new things. It allows me to travel throughout the world, and to learn about cultures I might otherwise never have been exposed to. It has forced me to look at people in ways I never would have otherwise, and offered me insight into why people wear what they do, which may be as intimate a revelation as there is (or so I like to tell myself). In fact, I often find a person's clothes more telling than what they say or do. And while it may not be easy to understand this intellectually, the process of anticipating consumers' desires is a tricky one. Over the years, I've learned to listen to the whispers of change, and take note of subtle nuances. Although I have missed plenty, fortunately I've been right more often than not, and learned that the process of anticipating change is more evolutionary than revolutionary, one that I am constantly reassessing.

"Some accessories just don't fly."
—Kenneth Cole

In the 1980s most of my thoughts changed as I started to hear from first-time greeters: "Kenneth Cole! I love your ads!" Leaving me muttering quietly, "Great, but what about my shoes?"

Far be it from me to run from a compliment, but sometime after Kenneth Cole Productions established a strong advertising voice, I realized that we were still just a shoe company. If we wanted to be a fashion company, something would have to change. We needed to not just sell clothes and accessories, but a lifestyle.

In fashion, the 1980s was a pivotal decade. A dynamic geographical and philosophical shift over fashion was occurring. Whereas fashion in the past had begun on the runways of Paris and Milan, moving to New York, Tokyo, and then the rest of the world, the new fashion was starting to emerge in other places. The business itself was changing, as clothing designers like

"Picture yourself in leather."
—Kenneth Cole

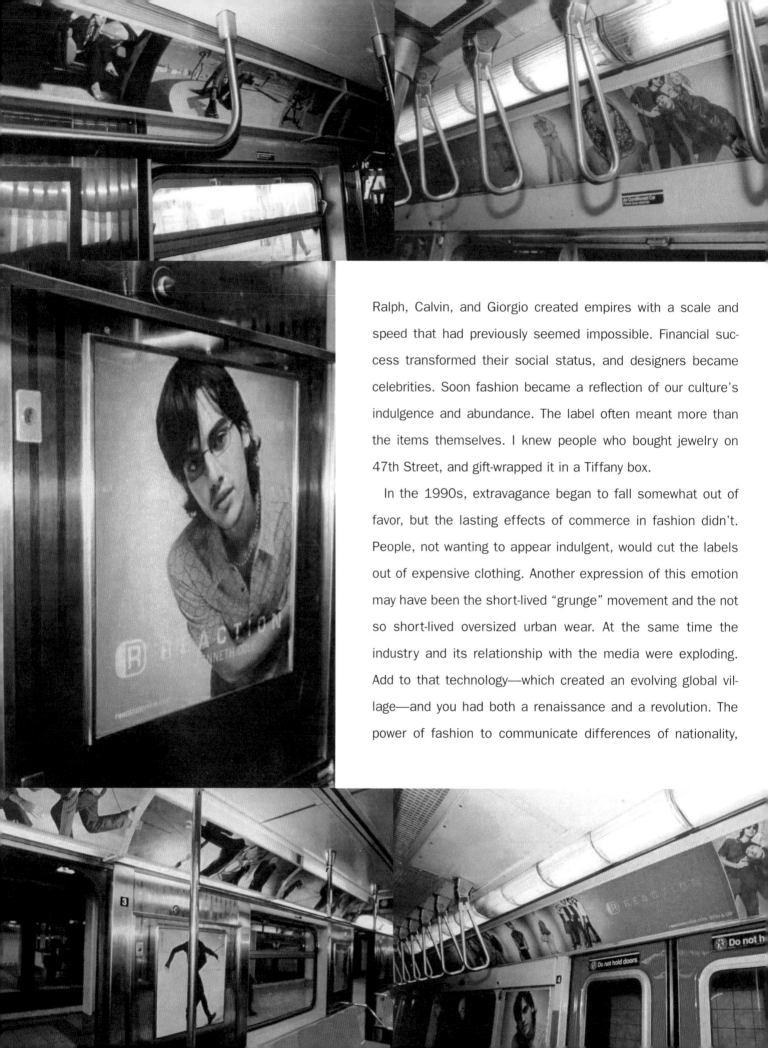

Ralph, Calvin, and Giorgio created empires with a scale and speed that had previously seemed impossible. Financial success transformed their social status, and designers became celebrities. Soon fashion became a reflection of our culture's indulgence and abundance. The label often meant more than the items themselves. I knew people who bought jewelry on 47th Street, and gift-wrapped it in a Tiffany box.

In the 1990s, extravagance began to fall somewhat out of favor, but the lasting effects of commerce in fashion didn't. People, not wanting to appear indulgent, would cut the labels out of expensive clothing. Another expression of this emotion may have been the short-lived "grunge" movement and the not so short-lived oversized urban wear. At the same time the industry and its relationship with the media were exploding. Add to that technology—which created an evolving global village—and you had both a renaissance and a revolution. The power of fashion to communicate differences of nationality,

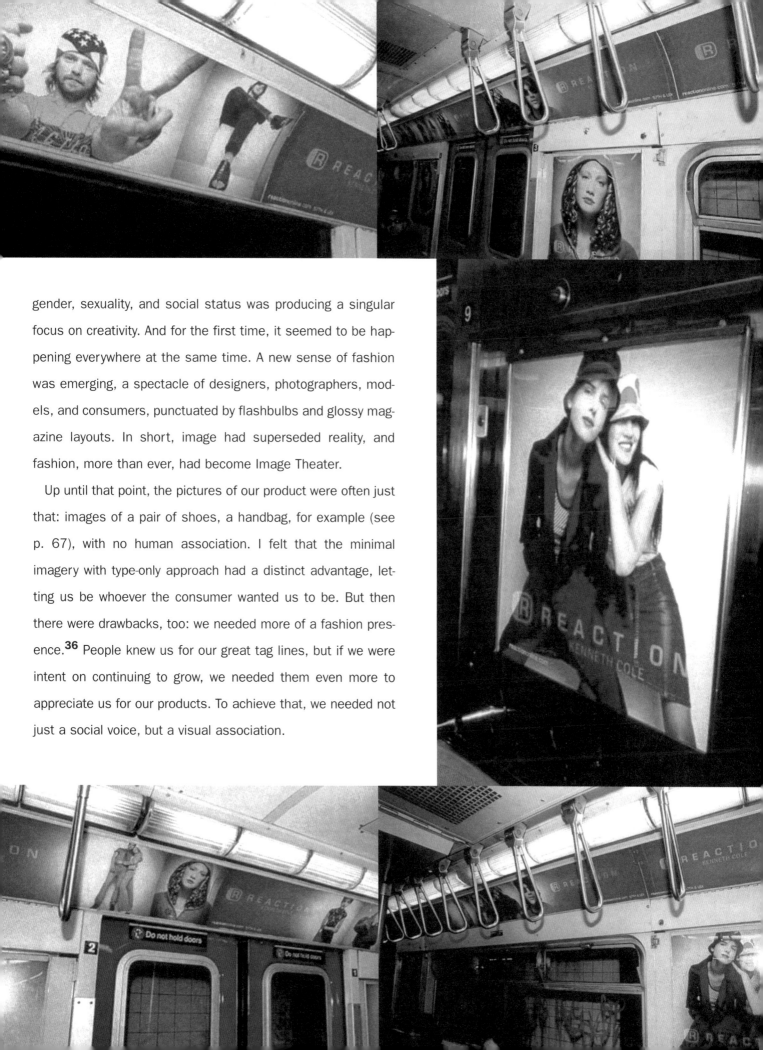

gender, sexuality, and social status was producing a singular focus on creativity. And for the first time, it seemed to be happening everywhere at the same time. A new sense of fashion was emerging, a spectacle of designers, photographers, models, and consumers, punctuated by flashbulbs and glossy magazine layouts. In short, image had superseded reality, and fashion, more than ever, had become Image Theater.

Up until that point, the pictures of our product were often just that: images of a pair of shoes, a handbag, for example (see p. 67), with no human association. I felt that the minimal imagery with type-only approach had a distinct advantage, letting us be whoever the consumer wanted us to be. But then there were drawbacks, too: we needed more of a fashion presence.[36] People knew us for our great tag lines, but if we were intent on continuing to grow, we needed them even more to appreciate us for our products. To achieve that, we needed not just a social voice, but a visual association.

194

FOOTNOTE #36
THE WRONG REACTION

When we launched a more urban/casual brand, Reaction, we hired photographer Terry Richardson to shoot one of our earliest campaigns that appeared exclusively in the New York subways. Unfortunately, I was shocked a few months later when an article appeared in the *New York Post* about someone who went into a rage over one of them: it was a photo of a man with women's ankles on either side of his head. Upon seeing it, the man began tearing it down, and ended up having a heart attack. **LESSON:** *Some reactions create the wrong reactions.*

JUST WHEN YOU THOUGHT IT WAS SAFE TO GO OUT IN THE SUBURBS...

I hadn't used models before because I never wanted to be associated with one kind of individual.

Enter the photographers, the models, the runway shows. I sought to offer a lifestyle, and to do that I needed to evolve our use of imagery.[37] We were learning how to marry images with our voice, reflecting popular economic and social trends season after season. A fashion statement is just that—a form of language that acknowledges something larger within our culture. It makes its way into the world via city streets, cul-de-sacs, small towns, and catwalks. A fashion statement, I've come to believe, takes all the cultural imagery of the world and synthesizes it into a common language that's accessible across social and geographic boundaries. It's a contemporary Esperanto, spoken more through images than words.

Communication of which came through expertly lit, styled photographs, through typographic formats, and through carefully chosen settings. In some years, our style may be pared-down, high-tech functionalism in primary colors; at other times the unexpected, large, clean surfaces and graphic simplicity of matte black. On the runways, we choose which faces and bodies best represent the clothes and the brand, putting them on real people with fantastic proportions and sending them down a sixty-foot plank, surrounded by the churning waters of fashion's finest.

I guess, if you happen to be looking these days, that is often where you might find me. I swim in this fashion aquarium, absorbing history, trends, and emotions and offering my own interpretation. Navigating these waters isn't always easy, but with the energy, insights, and inspiration of many friends, some of the industry's best, I've learned to better define who I am and what I want to be.[38]

The ultimate challenge remaining now is to evolve it without ever compromising the underlying mission. To offer and communicate a product and message that addresses how we appear on the outside without losing sight of who we are underneath. The ultimate fashion statement.

FOOTNOTE #37
"OVER EXPOSURE"?

We had further surprises in store when we made an effort to take urbanity to the suburbs. We hired a young camerawoman, then only twenty-four, to shoot a campaign featuring images of front yards, quiet streets, model Kirsten Owen, a baby, and a Ford Bronco with a bumper sticker that read "Life's a Bitch and Then You're Cloned."

I got quite a surprise that day when, during the shoot, I turned to look, and then looked again, noticing that the camerawoman had changed places with the model—and she was naked.

I came to learn that this wasn't the first time she photographed herself in the buff—al fresco. Since this one was on the set of a client, we got a little more of her than we bargained for. One of the ads she shot that day featured children playing on a lawn. When we later added a sign nearby that featured a marijuana leaf, and the slogan: "Keep off the Grass," she called repeatedly to object to the ad, as she was a proponent of marijuana for medicinal purposes. We were accomodating up to a point after all; she'd bared more than just her soul for us.

If you need a message, how about: *You can't tell a book by its cover.*

FOOTNOTE #38
ONE MAN'S TREASURE

Over the years, some very special friends have offered me great advice. Liz Tilberis, the late editor of *Harper's Bazaar*, used to tell me to "Be yourself." She told me to find my own style and stick with it, to have faith in my own vision.

Later, Anna Wintour, present editor of *Vogue*, friend, and mentor, offered this advice upon insistence: "Communicate. It's all good and fine for you to be yourself, but if we don't know who you are, we're hardly going to care. And try not to be all things to all people." Graydon Carter, editor of *Vanity Fair*, in his own light-hearted way, would remind me that it's just fashion and shouldn't be taken so seriously. There was also my friend Terry Lundgren, CEO of Federated Department Stores, who basically said, "Don't sell anything commercial to anyone but us." For me the message is: *the messages are relevant and still meaningful, but their value is relative to the intent of the messenger.*

unexpected

unlisted

It's the media's right to print what they see fit.
It's our right not to buy it.
—Kenneth Cole

conclusion

TWENTY YEARS LATER AND STILL SOLE-SEARCHING

Twenty years old. Twenty years of designing, taking risks, working fast, playing hard, and laughing in between. Twenty years of running into walls, imagining what might be behind them, and often taking the leap.

Taking the time for reflection necessary to write this book wasn't easy for me. No question about it, I'd rather be charging into the future than be bound to the past. I've always thought that drawn-out reflection was, at best, questionably relevant, at worst self-indulgent and a waste of time. But just recently, while pursuing my new passion of snowboarding, I had an accident that left me staring up at the ceiling of an ICU in Vail, Colorado, for five days. I had no choice but to reflect and to acknowledge how extraordinarily lucky I have been in both my professional and personal lives.

Some days I feel like I'm taking the bull by the horns, and others like I'm hanging on for the ride of my life. And though I spend much of my time struggling to hold on to what I have, while simultaneously pushing to move forward, life is never boring. The truth is, I have never spent any two days in my entire career doing the same thing. I don't know another business in which every day is different from the last and the next, where surprises are par for the course, and new challenges arise at every turn.

This company has been a team effort since its inception, and without the support of my family, colleagues, and friends, I wouldn't have been able to make it past the first hurdle, let alone a lifetime of

"Sole searching?"
—Kenneth Cole

leaps. Let there be no doubt, I am very proud of the company I keep—no pun intended (for once!).

In my daily existence, I am always both in the forest and ten thousand feet above it at all times, or so it seems. I never had a long-term plan for the business until Wall Street came along, believing that a long-term strategy in fashion was an oxymoron. I have learned so much since then. At Kenneth Cole Productions, we have recognized the need to build an organization that is able to turn, adapt, and change as often as necessary. We have learned the meaning of compromise and the benefit of giving back.

I have had the privilege of being able to play a small part in the way many people look on the outside, and hopefully, how they feel on the inside as well. It is an accomplishment that I am very proud of, and a privilege that I take very seriously. I look forward to earning it for years to come.

So now the book comes to an end, the story of the beginning through the middle, and I'm off to explore new pastures, by airplane or snowboard or just by foot. I'm off to seek out what is new and timely—and in that way I guess I'm not that much different from most kids my age.

What's going to happen next? I can't tell you. Anything could be around the corner: a sea of change, a world of possibility, or just something a little unexpected. For the time being, I'll keep on going, one step at a time. Because (and for my final pun) . . . the shoe must go on.

Sole Survivors.
—Kenneth Cole

ACKNOWLEDGMENTS

I am so appreciative to so many for so much.

Maria, my wife, who has always supported and challenged me, and who first had the idea for this book. A great partner, and a great mother of our three children, who, with her boundless energy, is all the while an inspiring role model.

To my daughters, Emily, Amanda, and Catie, who mean everything to me. They have taught me so much about what matters, what doesn't, as well as how to download music from the Internet.

Maybe no one more than my father, Charles Cole, who had he still been with us, would have been more proud today than anyone. He took extraordinary pleasure in all of my early successes whether sanctioned or not. He had a wonderful spirit and outlook, and his glass was never less than half full.

And to my mother, who was and still is the eternal anchor for us all. My brothers, Neil and Evan, and sister, Abbie, who, along with other family members, have shared many of the benefits as well as the burdens of this journey.

To all of my associates, many of whom have been with me for ten years or more, and have spent most of their professional careers committed to a shared vision. They have worked tirelessly so that this story could come to be, and so that I could take the time to write it. There are so many that if I tried to list them all here, I wouldn't know where to stop. They do the work for which I often get the credit.

To my friends and extended family who have always been by my side, and often make a point of wearing my clothes as a show of support, whether they fit or not, and who tolerate my sometimes questionable attempts at humor.

My gratitude also goes to those who excel at the painstaking process of editing and collaboration on a book: Rock Brynner, who patiently edited every step, Amanda Murray for her guidance, Mira Jacob for her tolerance and writing assistance, Yolanda Cuomo for her art direction and extraordinary patience, and Nan Richardson and Umbrage Editions for getting the project off the ground.

Special thanks to certain friends and family who found valuable time to help with aspects of this book: Brian O'Donoghue, my brother-in-law, who was always available and didn't mind all the puns; David Brenner, an old friend (who did mind), for his humor; friend Lisa Birnbach, as well as the invaluable assistance of my associates Leslie Kolk and Kristin Hoppmann, who helped pull it all together.

PHOTO CREDITS

SIMON & SCHUSTER
Rockefeller Center
1230 Avenue of the Americas
New York, NY 10020

For information regarding special discounts for bulk purchases,
please contact Simon & Schuster Special Sales at
1-800-456-6798 or business@simonandschuster.com

Associate book designer: Kristi Norgaard
Cover design: Christopher M. Yoham
Production assistant: Natalya Yamrom

Manufactured in Hong Kong

1 3 5 7 9 10 8 6 4 2

Library of Congress Cataloging-in-Publication Data

Cole, Kenneth.
    Footnotes / Kenneth Cole.
        p. cm
    1. Advertising—Fashion. 2. Kenneth Cole Productions. I. Title.

HF6161.C44C65 2003
659.1'9687—dc21   2003050565

ISBN 0-7432-4177-0

Book design by
YOLANDA CUOMO DESIGN, NYC

IT'S GREAT TO
BE KNOWN FOR YOUR
SHOES, BETTER
TO BE KNOWN FOR
YOUR SOLE

IT'S OK TO BE CLOTHES MINDED • WE SUPPORT ARTISTIC FREEDOM AND CREATIVE

SHIRT HAPPENS • 55% OF SOCIETY BELIEVES THE MEDIA SHOULD FOCUS ON REAL

TO BE AWARE IS MORE IMPORTANT THAN WHAT YOU WEAR • 81% OF AMERIC

WITHOUT MENTORS, KIDS ARE 80% MORE LIKELY TO BECOME SOMETHING IN LIFE

SOLE SEARCH • 1 IN 27 PEOPLE EXECUTED IN THE U.S. IS PROVEN INNOCENT OVER

ALMOST AS MANY SUITS ARE TRIED IN THE COURTROOM TODAY AS THE DRESSING ROOM

40% OF AMERICANS BELIEVE CLONING A SHEEP IS UNETHICAL, ALTHOUGH 65% CH

REGARDLESS OF THE RIGHT TO BEAR ARMS, WE IN NO WAY CONDONE THE RIGHT

65% OF AMERICANS HAVE MORE SUCCESS MAKING THEIR OUTFIT WORK T

WE SUPPORT ARTISTIC FREEDOM AND CREATIVE LICENSE, BUT DRAW THE LINE

STAND FOR SOMETHING OR STEP ASIDE • SOME STATEMENTS ARE MORE FASHIONA

TO BE AWARE IS MORE IMPORTANT THAN WHAT YOU WEAR • 81% OF AMERIC

WITHOUT MENTORS, KIDS ARE 80% MORE LIKELY TO BECOME SOMETHING IN LIFE

SOLE SEARCH • 1 IN 27 PEOPLE EXECUTED IN THE U.S. IS PROVEN INNOCENT OVER

ALMOST AS MANY SUITS ARE TRIED IN THE COURTROOM TODAY AS THE DRESSING ROO

40% OF AMERICANS BELIEVE CLONING A SHEEP IS UNETHICAL, ALTHOUGH 65% CHE

REGARDLESS OF THE RIGHT TO BEAR ARMS, WE IN NO WAY CONDONE THE RIGHT TO B

39% OF WOMEN PREFER SHOE SHOPPING TO SEX • 65% OF AMERICANS HAVE M

WE SUPPORT ARTISTIC FREEDOM AND CREATIVE LICENSE, BUT DRAW THE LINE AT

SOME STATEMENTS ARE MORE FASHIONABLE THAN OTHERS • AVOID SPLINT

THE AVERAGE AMERICAN IS ONLY THREE PAYCHECKS AWAY FROM LOSING

WITHOUT MENTORS, KIDS ARE 80% MORE LIKELY TO BECOME SOMETHING IN LIFE.

THE AVERAGE WOMAN FALLS IN LOVE 7 TIMES A YEAR. ONLY 6 ARE WITH SHOES • A

67% OF KIDS TODAY HAVE ACCESS TO THE HOTTEST NEW ACCESSORY. THE FAMILY GU

40% OF AMERICANS BELIEVE CLONING A SHEEP IS UNETHICAL, ALTHOUGH 65% CH

IT'S OK TO BE CLOTHES MINDED • REGARDLESS OF THE RIGHT TO BEAR ARMS, WE IN NO